# DOES LIFE HAVE ANY MEANING?

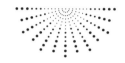

## JOHN BLANCHARD

# CONTENTS

**Published by EP BOOKS**

(Evangelical Press) 1st Floor Venture House, 6 Silver Court, Watchmead, Welwyn Garden City, UK, AL7 1TS

www.epbooks.org admin@epbooks.org

EP Books are distributed in the USA by:

JPL Distribution, 3741 Linden Avenue Southeast, Grand Rapids, MI 49548

www.jplbooks.com orders@jplbooks.com

**British Library Cataloguing in Publication Data available**

PRINT: ISBN 978-1-78397-227-2

eBOOK: ISBN 978-1-78397-228-9

# INTRODUCTION

The story is told of a policeman patrolling one of London's bridges over the River Thames when he saw a man climbing on to the railing. Pulling him back, the policeman asked him what he was doing. The man replied, 'I am going to drown myself, because there is nothing worth living for.' The policeman gradually calmed him down, then said, 'Let's talk about this. Tell me exactly why you feel that life has no meaning'—and when they had talked together for ten minutes they both jumped in...

The story may be no more than that, but the subject is seriously important. Searching for a meaning to life seems to be programmed into us as human beings. We may sometimes try to brush the subject aside, but time and again we still wonder whether there is any point in all our activities, experiences and emotions. Why are we here? What is life all about? Are we part of a bigger picture, or just specks of dust swirling around in a mindless universe?

One of America's best-known movie directors complained, 'If I had never lived, if the sperm that hit the egg had missed, it would have made no difference to anything.' Can we settle for that? Is there a road map that will help us to find our way through life—or are birth, life and death nothing more than isolated markers in a meaningless desert? Can we be sure that we are more important than peanuts or pilchards? Why do we claim to have any dignity or rights? Is doing so no more than pointless prattle?

If life has no meaning or purpose, what is the point of getting involved with the needs of other people? Why should we help those who are disabled, seriously ill, homeless, intellectually challenged, psychologically damaged or desperately poor? Why should we be concerned about the victims of war, genocide or persecution? If their lives are as meaningless as ours, what is the point of trying to help them?

These questions lead to others. Where can we find a basis for morality or responsible behaviour of any kind? On what basis can we differentiate between good and bad, right or wrong, fair or unfair? Can we sail through life without moral responsibility of any kind? If we are nothing more than biological accidents, cobbled together from bits of our ancestors, what is the point in speaking about human values or the quality of life? These are big questions, and it makes no sense to ignore them.

It has been said that the two most important days in your life are the day you are born and the day you find out why. This book aims at helping you to focus on the second.

# THE RESTLESS SEARCH

*I*n *Hair: The American Tribal Love-Rock Musical* the song 'Where Do I Go?' asks,

> *Why do I live, why do I die?*
> *Where do I go?*
> *Tell me why, tell me where?*
> *Tell me why, tell me where?*
> *Tell me why?*

People have been asking questions like these for as far back as we have been able to dig into our history but they have a long shelf life. Yet the search goes on, and the questions we asked in the Introduction keep on raising their heads. The British author Andrew Knowles underlines this: 'Am I really a random coincidence, adrift in a cosmic accident, meaning nothing, going nowhere? Surely I have a dimension that animals and vegetables lack? After all, a carrot is oblivious of the size of Jupiter. A cow cares nothing for the speed of light. But I am in a different class. I observe and appreciate. I create and choose. I criticize. Sometimes I even criticize myself.'

There are times in our high-tech, fast-moving world when

physical, mental, moral or financial pressures drive people to ask, 'What is the point of it all?' 'How long can I take this?' 'Why should I bother?' For some people, even significant achievers, the meaning of life depends on their emotions. The British explorer and adventurer Sir Ranulph Fiennes, was the first man to reach both the North Pole and the South Pole by surface, and climbed to the summit of Mount Everest when he was sixty-five years old. Asked for the meaning of life, he replied, 'To me life has many meanings depending what mood I'm in at the time,' but does that make sense? A person for whom everything is going well may give a positive and optimistic answer, but what answer might we get from a harassed housewife overwhelmed by family responsibilities, a businessman fighting a losing battle in the rat race, a person who has just been told they have terminal cancer, a man whose wife and children have died in a car crash, a married couple getting further into debt every month, a drug-dependent teenager, an alcoholic, a homeless refugee, or someone in prison for a crime they never committed? Their mood may indicate how they *feel*, but it tells us nothing about what their lives mean. The Australian journalist Jon Casimir may have been on to something when he said that looking for a meaning to life is like 'trying to find a lost sock in the cosmic laundromat.'

## SUCCESS AND FAILURE

Countless people envy their media-promoted heroes and imagine that matching their success (and bank balance) would bring lasting meaning to their lives, but the facts destroy the fantasy. *TIME* magazine called the American bestselling author, financial adviser, fundraiser and motivational speaker Suze Orman one of the world's most influential people. Yet when the author of *The 9 Steps to Financial Freedom* had become so wealthy that she could take holidays on a private island she said, 'I had more affluence than I'd ever dreamt of. Yet I felt sad and empty—and at a loss. For if money didn't equal happiness, I had no idea what did.'

Shortly before he died of an AIDS-related disease, the Tanzanian-born British musician Freddie Mercury, hailed as one of the greatest popular singers of all time, admitted, 'You can have everything in the world and still be the loneliest man, and that is the most bitter type of loneliness.' The lyrics of Queen's song 'The Show Must Go On' include the question, 'Does anybody know what we are living for?'

Many other high achievers underline the point that finding ultimate meaning and purpose in life is not a matter of health, success, wealth, popularity or pleasure. The fundamental mistake that countless people make is to pin the meaning of life to whatever works for them, or at least to whatever produces a feel-good factor; life is simply to be soaked up and enjoyed. Is it sensible to settle for this? If so, how can we claim that our lives have any greater meaning than those of cows, cockroaches or camels? When a person's life is so self-centred, what they see is all they get. The American television and social media personality Kim Kardashian makes the bizarre claim that issuing daily photographs of herself on Instagram is for her 'the purpose of life'. One hardly knows whether to laugh or cry.

# YOUR CHOICE?

*T*he British theoretical physicist and cosmologist Stephen Hawking was widely regarded as one of the most brilliant scientists since the world-famous physicist Albert Einstein. Although suffering from motor neurone disease, his ground-breaking work influenced countless people both inside and outside of academic and scientific circles.

Despite losing his voice permanently following a tracheotomy, his brilliant adaptations to cope with his growing disability led the Canadian physicist Werner Israel to compare his achievements to Mozart composing an entire symphony in his head. Before he died in March 2018, virtually all control of his body had gone and for vocal communication he directed a computerized voice system through a cheek muscle attached to a sensor. Though never complaining, he said, 'The downside of my celebrity is that I can't go anywhere without being recognized. It is not enough for me to wear sunglasses and a wig. The wheelchair gives me away.' Some people are merely famous for being famous; Stephen Hawking earned his fame.

## THE GOD QUESTION

One of his most popular books is *A Brief History of Time*, first published in 1988. In it, he tackles issues that directly relate to the question of whether life on our planet has any meaning. These include, 'How did the universe begin—and what made its start possible?' 'Does time always flow forward?' 'Is the universe unending—or are there boundaries?' 'Are there other dimensions in space?' and 'What will happen when it all ends?' He flirts with the idea of 'A Theory of Everything' (TOE), one that would fully explain and link together all the physical aspects of the universe. This leads him to ask, 'Even if there is one possible unified theory, it is just a set of rules and equations. What is it that breathes fire into the equations and makes a universe for them to describe?'

He toys with the idea that the universe might have had a creator, and in the second edition of the book takes this a little further: 'It would be very difficult to explain why the universe should have begun in just this way, except as an act of a God who intended to create beings just like us.' He then gets to the question we are asking in the book you are now reading: 'We find ourselves in a bewildering world. We want to make sense of what we see around us and to ask: what is the nature of the universe? *What is our place in it, and where did it and we come from?*'

This left open for him the possibility that the meaning of life is to be found not in ourselves, or even in the natural world, but in a Creator who brought us and it into existence. However, twenty-two years later he took a very different line in *The Grand Design*, co-authored with the American physicist and screenwriter Leonard Mlodinow (who also worked on the science fiction television series *Star Trek: The Next Generation)*. The book begins by asking questions such as, 'How does the universe behave?', 'What is the nature of reality?', 'Where did all this come from?' and 'Did the universe need a Creator?' It then goes on to say that 'Because there is a law such as gravity, the universe can and will create itself from nothing.' This would rule God out of the picture, and Hawking does this by claiming that in looking for a reason why we and the universe exist, 'It is not necessary to invoke God to light the blue touch-paper.'

## THE PROGRAMME

In a Discovery HD television programme *The Meaning of Life*, Hawking told viewers, 'We humans are a curious species. We wonder. We seek answers. So can we answer the greatest question of all: *is there a meaning to life?*' This set the stage for a brilliant production, bursting with colour, wrapped in richly textured music, and featuring space photography, dazzling computer-generated graphics and time-lapse sequences, as well as a kaleidoscope of scenes ranging from brain surgery to a boating trip.

In the course of the programme, Hawking said, 'We all have hopes and dreams, but the first thing we must accept as we search for the meaning of life is that this is *nothing more than physics.*' This led him to wonder, 'If we are just biological clockwork, perhaps there is no meaning to life—perhaps no meaning at all.' Yet rather than leave it suspended in mid-air, he went on to say, 'The entire 13.7 billion-year history of the universe exists as a model inside our minds. So where does this leave us with finding a meaning to life? The answer I think is pretty clear. Meaning itself is simply another piece of the model of reality that we build inside our own brain. Love and honour, right and wrong are all part of the universe we create in our minds.'

Then came the programme's punchline: *'The meaning of life is what you choose it to be.'*

At first glance this seems a perfectly reasonable idea— until we begin to think it through. As there are presently over seven billion people living on our planet, does this mean that there could be as many as seven billion different answers to the question, and that none of them is more reliable than personal opinion, which could change several times a day?

# GOD'S UNDERTAKER?

$\mathcal{I}$n claiming that the laws of physics point to the meaning of life, Hawking joins with those who claim that science can not only explain everything we need to know about the physical universe, but that it also buries God and stamps on his grave. In doing this, the well-known British biologist Richard Dawkins wields one of the biggest spades: 'I think science really has fulfilled the need that religion did in the past, of explaining things, explaining why we are here, what is the origin of life, where did the world come from, what life is all about… Science has the answers.'

If he is right, we can ignore the God question—but is he? His first claim is that science can explain *why we are here*; but it can do no such thing. Even a passionate atheist like the Welsh geneticist Steve Jones admits, 'Science cannot answer the question, "Why are we here?"' The second claim is that science can explain *the origin of life*. Not only is this untrue, but not even the world's leading scientists can agree on what life *is*. *Encyclopedia Britannica* ends a long article on the subject by saying, 'There is no generally accepted definition of life,' and science can only offer wild guesses as to how life got here in the first place. The third claim is that science can explain *where the world came from*. We will dig into this in the next chapter, but to claim that science can explain the world's existence goes far beyond the facts, and for the British scientist Peter Atkins to call it 'an elaborate and engaging re-arrangement of nothing' in which 'space-time generates its own dust in the process of its own self-assembly' gets us nowhere. The fourth claim is that science can explain *what life is all about*, yet on another occasion, when *The Observer* asked Dawkins about the purpose of life he replied, 'Well, there is no purpose, and to ask what it is is a silly question.'

At this point, we need to make something crystal clear: *statements by scientists are not necessarily scientific statements.* There are times when they are no more than personal opinions that may be driven by a predetermined agenda and coloured by prejudices or preferences, rather than being based on solid facts.

A good example of this is Dawkins claiming elsewhere, 'Religion is no longer a serious candidate in the field of explanation. It is completely superseded by science.' If this is true, there is no point in bringing God into the picture when looking for the meaning of life; but in saying this Dawkins is shuffling the cards under the table and producing not science but *scientism*, which is something very different. Simply put, scientism (sometimes called materialism or naturalism) says that everything can be reduced to a scientific explanation of its parts. This is why it is often called reductionism, though I prefer the term coined by the Scottish physicist and brain scientist Donald MacKay, who dubbed it 'nothing-buttery.' This says that the whole universe, and everyone and everything in it, is 'nothing but' matter and energy driving atoms and molecules. This is a neat way of pinpointing scientism's claim that it is the only show in town, and that even human beings, the most complex and amazing creatures we know, are just collections of biological bits and pieces, and when we have identified these, and described how they work, we have discovered all that can be said about us.

This obviously has a direct bearing on the question this book is asking. If as human beings we are merely accumulations of atoms and molecules arranged in a certain way, how can we know that there is any meaning to life? Which of these chemical and biological elements tells us whether we have any value, significance or purpose?— especially if Dawkins is right in saying that we came into existence 'by a blind, unconscious, automatic process' that had 'no purpose in mind.' Scientism is not science, but a particular philosophy *about* science, and is of no help whatever in trying to find an answer to the question this book is asking.

Science is the ongoing process of discovering truth in the natural world, but time and again scientists tell us that previously accepted theories and hypotheses can be rejected, as they have been replaced by others that are more credible. True science relies on observation and experiment, and nobody can deny the phenomenal contributions that science and technology continue to make to human life on this planet. They combine to revolutionize our lives, but the claim that science is the only way to discover truth about the universe and the meaning of human life is ignorance masquerading as intelligence, as there are many massively important things that are beyond the reach of science and the scientific method. As the Nobel Prize-winning British biologist Sir Peter Medawar put it, 'There is no quicker way for a scientist to bring discredit upon himself and upon his profession than roundly to declare…that science knows, or will soon know, the answers to all questions worth asking.' Here are three areas directly relating to the meaning of life in which science can give us no answers.

The first is that *science is unable to explain why we are persons and not just physical objects.* In February 2001 the Human Genome Project unveiled its landmark report spelling out the three billion letters that make up the human genome. The British physician and medical journalist James Le Fanu acknowledged that it was an 'impressive achievement', but also 'devastating news' for scientists who had promised that it would reveal all we needed to know about ourselves: 'The holy grail, the dream that science would soon tell us something significant about what it means to be human, has slipped through our hands—and we are no wiser than before. *The human genome... can tell us absolutely nothing about the really important things in life.*'

The second is that *science is unable to explain why the mind exists and functions as it does.* When we want to find whether life has any meaning, we use our minds to pull together all the factors we think might be relevant. We reflect on past experience, we assess where we are at present, we think about what the future might hold, and we wonder whether we fit into a bigger picture. Yet as the British biochemist Arthur Peacocke pointed out, 'Science can investigate all the physical aspects of the brain, but there is still something about the mind—and therefore about who you really are—that it cannot get at.'

The third is that *science is unable to explain ethical principles.* These come into the frame whenever we give serious thought as to whether life has any meaning, but while science can study the results of human behaviour, it can say nothing about what drives it. Things such as our concern for truth, virtue, justice and goodness show that we are more than what someone called 'computers made of meat'—yet science can tell us nothing about these hugely important things. It is even unable to tell us the difference between right and wrong—or why we should choose one rather than the other.

Nothing in this chapter should be taken as a criticism of science. Science is a stupendous success story, and growing more successful by the day, but there is no point in pretending that it can explain everything, including the meaning of life. Nor can it rule God out of the picture by (as Dawkins puts it) 'fulfilling the need that religion did in the past.' It is sometimes argued that as God cannot be proved by any scientific hypothesis we can assume he does not exist, but it is easy to demolish this argument. The very statement, 'God cannot be proved by any scientific hypothesis' cannot be proved by any scientific hypothesis. Does this mean that the statement does not exist? In the course of an Oxford

University Debate, Peter Atkins let the cat out of the bag. Before letting fly with both barrels at religion in general and Christianity in particular he inserted this significant escape clause: 'I have to admit from the outset that science cannot disprove the existence of God.'

# 4
## MOLECULES TO MAN?

$\mathcal{O}$ne obvious approach in looking for the meaning of human life would be to ask a very basic question: 'How did we get here?' This is the answer given by Stephen Jay Gould, one of the world's most frequently quoted scientists on the subject:

'We are here because one odd group of fishes had a peculiar fin anatomy that could transform into legs for terrestrial creatures; because the earth never froze entirely during an ice age; because a small and tenuous species, arising in Africa a quarter of a million years ago, has managed, so far, to survive by hook and by crook. *We may yearn for a "higher" answer, but none exists.*'

This was Gould's explanation of how human life came to exist on one tiny planet in a vast universe almost all of which is beyond our reach—and he signed off by insisting that no other explanation is possible or necessary. In doing this he is taking a small chunk out of a much bigger idea on which millions of people are relying to shape their thinking, not only about themselves but about the world around them: The Theory of Evolution. This covers so much that before we go any further we need to distinguish between its two different forms.

Biologists divide animals and other living things into categories. One of these lists domains, kingdoms, phyla, classes, orders, families, genera and species. Nobody seriously questions the fact that over time natural changes take place within the 'lower' of these categories (families, genera and species), often as a result of adaptation to a new environment. These changes can result in huge variations in the size, colour and other characteristics of the living things concerned. This phenomenon is commonly called *micro-evolution*. We can even manipulate or accelerate these changes by cross-breeding or by the genetic engineering of animals such as dogs, horses and birds—but however big the changes *they remain dogs, horses and birds.* For this reason 'variation' might be a better word to use than 'micro-evolution.'

The *macro-evolution* theory takes things much further, and says that all the world's life-forms are linked by a seamless process of spontaneous, random, natural means, without any external, intelligent power, going all the way back to a single spark of life that appeared on our planet at some point in prehistory. Richard Dawkins puts human beings into the picture by saying, 'It is the plain truth that we are cousins of chimpanzees, somewhat more distant cousins of monkeys, more distant cousins still of aardvarks and manatees, yet more distant cousins of bananas and turnips.' Elsewhere he added kangaroos, jellyfish and bacteria to the list.

The evolution revolution was largely kicked off by the British naturalist and geologist Charles Darwin with the 1859 publication of *The Origin of Species by Means of Natural Selection or the Preservation of Favoured Species*, now known as *The Origin of Species* or simply *The Origin*. He called micro-evolution his 'special theory,' but this was neither new nor controversial. What really hit the headlines was what he called his 'general theory,' which said that all species could be traced back to a single common ancestor (though the word 'evolution' did not appear in the book). This idea was so revolutionary that even Darwin admitted he often had 'grave misgivings' about it and was 'plagued with doubt' when qualified critics gave the book a hostile reception. But twelve years later he went even further and in *The Descent of Man* said that human beings were also the result of macro-evolution and had descended from 'some less highly organized form.' This completes the macro-evolution picture, telling us that every living thing we see, from a duck-billed platypus to a blade of grass, and from a great white shark to a housefly is part of our human family tree.

Darwin hedged his ideas around with so many questions that phrases like 'we may suppose' occur over 800 times in *The Origin of Species* and *The Descent of Man,* but his theory is now promoted so strongly in the media and elsewhere that it is taken for granted as giving an accurate description of how human beings came into existence. Richard Dawkins claims that macro-evolution is 'about as much open to doubt as the theory that the earth goes round the sun' and says it is absolutely safe to say that 'if you meet somebody who claims not to believe in evolution, that person is ignorant, stupid or insane.' He even goes so far as to describe such people as 'history-deniers.'

With the massive endorsement evolution receives in political, educational and media circles, two obvious questions need to be asked and answered. The first is whether the macro-evolution theory is true; and the second is whether it is the elusive key to unlocking the meaning of life. Looking at the first of these questions will take up most of the rest of this chapter; a few lines will answer the second.

## DARWIN'S POND

Before evolution of any kind can take place there obviously has to be a living organism to get the ball rolling. In trying to find this starting point, Darwin imagined that there might have been 'some warm little pond, with all sorts of ammonia and phosphoric salts, light, heat, electricity, etc. present,' together with 'a protein compound chemically formed ready to undergo still more complex changes.' This was nothing more than guesswork, and today we are no better equipped in trying to locate what is usually called pre-biotic 'soup' (some kind of fluid existing before the emergence of life). How could it have got there in the first place? How could it have contained the elements Darwin had in mind? Could it all have come together in the course of what Peter Atkins called 'an elaborate and engaging re-arrangement of nothing'? These are fascinating questions, but one simple fact makes them all hypothetical: *there is not a shred of evidence to prove that this pre-biotic soup ever existed.*

The next step in examining the macro-evolutionary model is to ask how it gets from inanimate chemicals to a life form—in other words, moves from lifeless soup to the first living cell. The step becomes even more difficult when we realize that bacterial cells, the simplest we know of, are far more complicated than any machine ever built. They have thousands of exquisitely inter-related and compatible items of molecular machinery made up of millions of atoms, all using the same genetic code as all other cells, including those in human beings. To give one specific example, *Mycoplasma genitalium*, the bacterium with the smallest known amount of genetic information, has 580,000 base pairs in its 482 genes.

We also know that all the DNA data needed to specify the design of a complete human being is packed into a unit weighing less than a few thousand-millionths of a gram, and is several thousand million million times smaller than the smallest piece of functional machinery ever devised. The DNA coding staggers the imagination. It has been said that it would take a stack of books that would encircle the earth 5,000 times to contain the information in a mere pinhead of DNA. Another estimate suggests that all the information needed to specify the design of every living species that has ever existed on our planet could be put into a teaspoon, with enough room left over for the digital contents of every book ever written.

Although countless experiments have been conducted to see how it might have been possible for the first spark of life to have been generated by lifeless chemicals, the most anyone has done is to produce a few amino acids, which are almost infinitely less complex than the simplest protein molecules essential for life. The bottom line here is that neither the random flow of energy through primordial soup, nor any other unguided and mindless process, could ever lead to even the most primitive organism. To say that life somehow arose from non-life is on a par with saying that something accidentally arose from nothing. The distinguished British astronomer Sir Fred Hoyle (who coined the term 'The Big Bang') dismissed the issue like this: 'The likelihood of the formation of life from inanimate matter is 1 to a number with 40,000 noughts after it… It is big enough to bury Darwin and the whole theory of evolution.' To emphasize his point, he asked us to imagine a vast number of blind people, each with a scrambled Rubik's cube, all solving the problem simultaneously, before adding, 'You then have a chance of arriving by random shuffling at just one of the many biopolymers on which life depends. The notion that not only the biopolymers but the operating program of a living cell could be arrived at by chance in a primordial organic soup here on the Earth is evidently nonsense of a high order.'

The next roadblock the theory of evolution faces is the fact that the first single-celled organism would need to have been completely self-contained, including whatever it needed to write its own software. Richard Dawkins admits, 'Nobody knows how it happened, but somehow, without violating the laws of physics and chemistry, a molecule arose that just happened to have the property of self-copying.' He calls this a 'replicator'—but confesses that the odds against this are 1 in 'an exceedingly large number, far greater than the number of fundamental particles in the universe.' Surely this is closer to science fiction than to science?

## THE THEORY

In spite of this, we are told that this self-replication gradually went into overdrive, with successive evolutionary changes gradually adding to the fantastic complexity of the living organisms we now see. To summarize this in a single paragraph, it is said that although over many millions of years the first single-celled organisms were all invertebrates, that is to say they had no spinal column or backbone, this was to change. After hundreds of millions of years, invertebrates became vertebrates, of which there are now over 60,000 species. In another thirty million years these evolved into amphibians (capable of living on land as well as in water) of which there are now some 7,000 species, including frogs, toads, newts and salamanders. These eventually evolved into reptiles, such as snakes, lizards, crocodiles and tortoises. Then, over millions more years, some of these evolved into birds; those without legs developed them and all of them added wings. Birds then evolved into four legged, furry animals, from which ape-like mammals came into being. These evolved into apes, then finally into humans. Millions of people take this fascinating theory for granted, so that in the American television premiere of *Ape Man: The Story of Human Evolution,* the presenter told viewers, 'If you go back far enough, we and the chimps share a common ancestor. My father's father's father's father, going back maybe half a million generations—about five million years—was an ape.'

This scenario says that if genes underwent radical changes (mutations), natural selection could make use of the best of them and, given sufficient time, could produce new and better forms. It is said that the survival of these could, for example, explain an ape or ape-like creature evolving into a human being. Yet this idea ignores some important facts. The first is that natural mutations occur only once in something like ten million duplications of a DNA molecule. The second is that 999 out of every 1,000 duplications are harmful, weakening or destroying the organism concerned, rather than leading to an improvement. As biologist Lynn Margulis, once a member of the US National Academy of Sciences, confirms, 'New mutations don't create new species; they create offspring that are impaired.'

The third is that the difference between apes and humans represents about 150 million units of additional information — *yet nobody has ever found a single case of a mutation adding any information.* The American biophysicist Lee Spetner tells us what this means: 'Whoever thinks macro-evolution can be made by mutations that lose information is like the merchant who lost a little money on every sale but thought he could make it up on volume... The failure to observe even one mutation that adds information is more than just a failure to find support for the theory. It is evidence against the theory.'

## FROM MOLECULES TO MEANING?

The question of whether macro-evolution is the key to our finding whether human life has any meaning or purpose is easily answered. If we are merely accidental, unguided collections of biological bits and pieces that had no intelligent aim in mind, how can we even imagine that life might have any meaning? Macro-evolution reduces everything to nature and natural processes, and can give humankind no higher status than that of an accidental by-product of laws with no rational or moral dimension. William Provine says that the message of modern evolutionary biology is 'loud and clear': 'There are no gods, no purposes, no goal-directing forces of any kind... There is no ultimate foundation for ethics, *no meaning to life.'*

To find out whether there is one, we will need to look elsewhere.

# 5

# COSMIC CLUES

    Space is big. Really big. You just won't believe how vastly, hugely mind-bogglingly big it is. I mean, you may think it's a long way down the road to the chemist, but that's just peanuts to space.

*T*hese may be the best-known words in the British author Douglas Adams' multi-media phenomenon *The Hitchhiker's Guide to the Galaxy*—and he can hardly be accused of exaggerating. If planet Earth was the size of the full-stop at the end of this sentence, the moon would be five-eighths of an inch away, the sun just over nineteen feet and the nearest star 1005 miles. Those numbers and proportions are staggering enough, but like that trip to the chemist they are 'peanuts.' Keeping to the same scale, we would still be 467,600,000 miles from the Andromeda Galaxy. Yet this is the nearest galaxy to ours (the Milky Way). The Extreme Deep Field (XDF) image obtained by the Hubble Space Telescope suggests there are at least 200 billion other galaxies in the known universe, stretching out some fourteen billion light years (a light year is about six trillion miles) from Earth in every direction. Two hundred years ago most scientists believed that the Milky Way was the entire universe and that only about 100 million stars existed. Today, we know differently—and space really is 'vastly, hugely mind-bogglingly big.' The sun, a million times the size of Earth, bears the same relation to the size of the known universe as a single grain of sand does to all the world's beaches. Every year, astronomers give us a fuller picture—early in 2017 NASA discovered seven new planets thirty-nine light years from Earth, adding to over 3,570 other planets found since 1992.

Nearly 300 years ago the German mathematician and philosopher Gottfried Leibniz asked a question that is as relevant today as it was then: '*Why is there something rather than nothing?*' This points to other questions we should ask if we are serious about discovering whether life on our planet has any meaning. How did the universe come into existence? Why is it the way it is? Do its amazing features, including the unique arrangement of stars, planets and galaxies, point to it having come into being by chance or accident, or to an intelligent creating power? Would the answers help us in our search for the meaning of life?

## A BEGINNING—OR NONE?

In *The Hitchhiker's Guide to the Galaxy* a superior race builds a supercomputer able to calculate the meaning of 'life, the universe and everything.' After seven-and-a-half million years it comes up with the answer: 42. When Douglas Adams was asked why he chose that number he replied that it was a joke: 'I sat at my desk, stared into the garden and thought: "42 will do." I typed it out. End of story.' Of course it is not, and we need to look at two of the best-known theories in response to Leibniz's question.

**The first is that the universe has always existed**, an idea that is generally called the Steady State Theory. The British philosopher Bertrand Russell claimed, 'There is no reason why the world could not have come into being without a cause; nor, on the other hand, is there any reason why it should not have always existed. There is no reason to suppose that the world had a beginning at all.' However, the Nobel Prize-winning American astrophysicist Arno Penzias easily knocks this idea on the head: 'The creation of the universe is supported by all the observable data astronomy has produced so far.' Discoveries made by the Hubble Space Telescope have also shown that the known universe is expanding outwards in every direction, with the galaxies moving farther and farther away from us and from each other.

This discovery triggered off a massive game-changer, because by rewinding the process and taking time backwards instead of forwards, astronomers could imagine the universe getting smaller and smaller, with the galaxies getting closer to each other and to us. Eventually, all the mass, energy, and space-time in the universe would have been compressed to an infinitely dense, dimensionless point, usually called a 'singularity.'

This fits perfectly with the Second Law of Thermodynamics, which (put at its very simplest) says that as the universe's available energy is 'running down' it must have begun in a highly ordered, energy-packed state. Albert Einstein had problems squaring this with his General Theory of Relativity, but after he had visited the Palomar Observatory at Mount Wilson, California and looked through its massive space telescope he told the media, 'I now see the necessity of a beginning.'

***The second idea is that the universe is self-created***. As we saw in Chapter 2, Stephen Hawking claims in *The Grand Design*, 'Because there is a law such as gravity, the universe can and will create itself from nothing.' He then goes on to say, 'Spontaneous creation is the reason there is something rather than nothing, why the Universe exists, why we exist.' If he is right, there can obviously be no meaning to life in any part of the universe, let alone on planet Earth, and there is no point in trying to find one—but there are four fundamental flaws in his bizarre claim.

*In the first place, it is self-contradictory.* It begins by giving credit for the creation of everything to the law of gravity, but then says that before there was anything there was 'nothing.' But how could the universe have been created out of nothing if self-creation depended on the law of gravity or any other laws to kick-start the process? To make a meal, we need ingredients, but if we start with nothing we will go hungry. Nothing exists unless something (or someone) brought it into existence, and beginning with 'nothing' gets us nowhere. This knocks the whole idea of self-creation on the head, as it means that the universe would have to be both something and nothing at the same time and in the same sense.

*Secondly*, as the British author C. S. Lewis pointed out, 'In the whole history of the universe the laws of nature have never produced a single event. They are the pattern to which every event must conform, provided only that it can be induced to happen... the source of events must be sought elsewhere.' Simply put, laws can never create anything. All they can do is record what happens, and why.

*Thirdly, the idea turns logic on its head*, because for something to create itself it would need to exist in order to do the creating. Bringing something into existence is an action (and in the case of the universe a mind-bogglingly big one!), but if the universe did not exist before it brought itself into existence how could it create anything, let alone itself? Since nothing can create itself, there has to be a first, uncreated cause.

*Fourthly, it clashes with the First Law of Thermodynamics* (sometimes known as the law of conservation of mass and energy) which says that while mass can be converted into energy, and energy into mass, it can neither be self-created nor totally destroyed.

Reviewing the Hawking television programme *A Brief History of Mine* in *The Daily Telegraph*, columnist Michael Deacon writes about trying to get his mind around Hawking's claim that the universe just came into existence all by itself. He explains that he found it 'a vain struggle' because 'If the universe just came into existence all by itself, that means that before the universe there was nothing. And if there was nothing, there were no materials with which to create the universe. Which means that…' One thing is certain: if the universe did come into existence 'all by itself' we are wasting our time looking for the meaning of life on one of its tiny planets.

The idea that 'nothing' produced our amazingly complex universe leads the British scholar Keith Ward, a Fellow of the British Academy, to ask some interesting questions: 'One day there might be nothing. The next day, there might be a very large carrot. Nothing else in existence whatsoever, all alone and larger than life, a huge carrot. If anything is possible, that certainly is. The day after that, the carrot might disappear and be replaced by a purple spotted gorilla. Why not? … Why does this thought seem odd, or even ridiculous, whereas the thought that some law of physics might just pop into existence does not? Logically, they are exactly on a par.'

The British physicist Paul Davies puts it like this: 'Modern physics has shown that there is something truly extraordinary about the way the laws of physics fit together. It is not just any old universe; it is a very special, fine-tuned arrangement of things.' He then adds, 'The laws of physics dovetail with such an exquisite consistency and coherence that *the impression of design is overwhelming.*' Elsewhere, with no religious agenda, he says, 'It is hard to resist the impression that the present structure of the universe, apparently so sensitive to minor alterations in the numbers, has been rather carefully thought out.'

### FINE-TUNED FACTS

It has long since been pointed out that if the depth of earth's oceans, the angle at which it is tilted on its axis (23.5 degrees), its rotational speed (just over 1000 miles an hour), its land-water ratio (30%-70%), its average distance from the sun (just under 93 million miles), and a number of other factors were not precisely as they are our planet could not sustain life of any kind, let alone human life. The conditions in our solar system as well as on our planet need to be just right. Without an atmosphere of oxygen, none of us would be able to breathe, and without oxygen there would be no water. Without water there would be no rainfall for our crops, and without hydrogen, nitrogen, sodium, carbon, calcium and phosphorous human life would not be possible.

These all exist in exactly the right proportions to sustain life on earth, and astronomers and others have discovered that they are all related to an amazing degree of fine-tuning in the universe. Could all of this be accidental? It has been said that if you covered the United States with small coins, one of them marked, piled so high that they reached to the moon, repeated this 1,000 times, then asked a blindfolded person to pick out the marked coin, the chances of them doing so at the first attempt would be the same as the possibility of the universe's fine-tuning being a fluke. The American physician-geneticist Francis Collins, best known for his leadership of the Human Genome Project, says that the chances of the fifteen physical constants (physical qualities generally believed to be universal in nature and constant in time) existing with precisely the right values to give us a stable universe is 'almost infinitesimal'. The Canadian astrophysicist Hugh Ross agrees, and estimates that the chances of human life originating in this scenario are less than one chance in a trillion trillion trillion trillion trillion trillion trillion trillion trillion trillion trillion trillion, odds 'defying the laws of probability.'

What has all of this got to do with our question about the meaning of life? *Everything!* There is growing evidence that intelligent life on earth demands a unique arrangement of stars, planets and galaxies—exactly the ones we know are in place. If the universe came into existence by chance or accident, how can we explain what we find? There can be no rhyme or reason to it, nor can there be any plan or purpose in it. Yet if there is no meaning in the existence of the universe, how can there be any meaning in life of any kind, let alone human life? Anything that sprang into life on our planet (or any other planet or star for that matter) would merely be adding to a series of meaningless accidents. As C. S. Lewis put it, 'Either there is significance in the whole process of things as well as in human activity, or there is no significance in human activity itself... You cannot have it both ways. If the world is meaningless, then so are we.'

Many people are attracted to the idea of a multiverse (or meta-universe), which suggests there is a finite or infinite number of universes (sometimes called parallel universes), but if this were true it would be of no help in answering our question about the meaning of life—it would just kick the can down the road. Humankind is the most advanced species we know, yet if its origin can be traced back to a countless series of universal accidents, seeking to give it any serious meaning is as futile as trying to make sense out of nonsense, or to say that 'xhyfcd' can be made to spell 'wheelbarrow.'

The cosmos has no scientific reason for existing, yet the universal, elegant and consistent laws of nature are amazingly and precisely suited to allow life on our planet. How can this be explained in natural terms? If all the elements in the universe are accidental and unconnected, how can human life have any meaning or purpose? If no meaning was put into the universe, none can ever be found there. We would therefore be spending our lives on a planet spinning at around 1,000 miles an hour and orbiting the sun at over 69,000 miles an hour, as part of a galaxy that is whirling through space at a vast speed in relation to other galaxies—and all to no purpose.

## CONNECTING THE CLUES

About 2,000 years ago the Roman philosopher Cicero wrote, 'What could be more clear or obvious when we look up to the sky and contemplate the heavens, than that there is some divinity or superior intelligence?' His understanding of the size and structure of the universe was very primitive compared to ours, but what he said points us to something very significant. Nearly 1,500 years later the Polish mathematician and astronomer Nicolaus Copernicus, who stunned the scientific world of his day by proving that the sun, rather than the earth, was at the centre of the universe, did the same thing when he said that our world 'has been built by the best and most orderly workman of all.'

Nobody was there to see the universe come into being, nor can we conduct any experiment that gets within light years of duplicating what took place. If it was created by an intelligent being our only way of knowing anything about it would be if this creator was to tell us. The British scientist Andrew Parker, selected by The Royal Institution in 2000 as one of the top eight in the nation to be a 'Scientist for the New Century,' is an evolutionary biologist who does not believe in God. Yet when he looked carefully at what the Bible says about creation he came to this conclusion: 'Without expecting to find anything, I discovered a whole series of parallels between the creation story on the Bible's first page and the modern, scientific account of life's history... The more detail is examined, the more convincing and remarkable I believe the parallels become... The opening page of Genesis [the first of the Bible's sixty-six books] is scientifically accurate but was written long before the science was known. How did the writer of this page come to write this creation account...? I must admit, rather nervously as a scientist averse to entertaining such an idea, that the evidence that the writer of the opening page of the Bible was divinely inspired is strong. I have never before encountered such powerful, impartial evidence to suggest that the Bible is the product of divine inspiration.'

If we rule out the idea that the universe is self-created or exists by chance, five things would be needed to bring it about —time, intelligence, energy, space and matter—and the Bible's opening words, in Genesis 1:1, 'In the beginning, God created the heavens and the earth' cover all five. There is no single word in Hebrew (the language in which that part of the Bible was originally written) that matches our English word 'universe', but *hassamayim we'et ha'ares* (translated 'the heavens and the earth') tells us that God created everything that exists outside of himself. In London's St Paul's Cathedral, the tomb of its architect Sir Christopher Wren, has the inscription, 'Reader, if you seek his monument, look around you.' The Bible says the same thing about God and the universe.

Believing this may seem like a massive step of faith, but is it a bigger step than to believe that the amazing harmony and beauty we see in the natural world is accidental, that life itself sprang into existence by chance, and that the vast amount of digital information in living things had no intelligent source? Active computers are not just hardware, they are driven by software, which needs a mind to design and write it. An orderly cosmos governed by such amazing laws needed an intelligent mind to put it together. Reflecting on the universe, the American scientist Allan Sandage, one of the twentieth century's most influential astronomers, stated, 'I find it quite improbable that such order came out of chaos. There has to be some organizing principle. God to me is a mystery but is the explanation for the mystery of existence—why there is something rather than nothing.'

Keith Ward had no doubt that God is 'the best final explanation there can be for the universe.' Any honest search for the meaning and purpose of life cannot rule him out.

# 6

## POINTERS

*W*e have seen that if the arrangement of stars, planets and galaxies is a gigantic fluke nothing on earth can have any purpose, nor can human life have any meaning. What is more, if the universe has no intelligent purpose behind it, neither does the human mind. Suggesting that the universe came about by chance gets us nowhere. Letting a bull loose in a china shop will not result in beautifully designed tableware, and giving chance a blank cheque produces rafts of questions, but no answers. The American theologian R. C. Sproul easily explains why the existence of the universe by chance can be ruled out: 'Chance is given credit for creating the universe. However, such a prodigious feat is beyond the capabilities of chance. Why? Chance can do nothing *because it is nothing.* Chance is merely a word that we use to explain mathematical possibilities. It is no thing. It has no power. It cannot produce, manage or cause anything because it is nothing.'

Could you be persuaded to believe that the book you are now reading had no author, publisher or printer? Are you even dabbling with the possibility that it suddenly (or slowly) came into existence out of nothing? Are you toying with the thought that all of its letters, words, sentences, paragraphs, pages and chapters fell into place by chance, and that the matching cover design sprang into being by accident? Every book has an author, every song has a composer, every painting has an artist, and every building has an architect; logic points to the universe having a creator. Far from being a haphazard collection of spatial junk, the universe is teeming with evidence of order and design. The American scientist Owen Gingerich, a senior Astronomer Emeritus at the Smithsonian Astrophysical Observatory, says, 'It seems to me that a universe that just is, and we happen to be here as part of this incredible, astonishing complexity without any sort of purpose or ultimate meaning makes it a sort of macabre joke and I find it difficult to accept that… it simply makes a lot more sense to me to think that somehow *there is ultimate purpose and reason behind it.'*

We can take this one step further. The universe might have been such that we could never get to grips with any of it, yet we find that our minds seem somehow to be in synch with the laws that govern it, and that they, in turn, are totally in tune with the internal software of our minds. As Albert Einstein put it, 'The most incomprehensible thing about the world is that it is comprehensible.' This is more than a hint that a vast intelligence has brought the universe into being for a purpose *and that that purpose includes us.* In 1973, the Australian theoretical physicist Brandon Carter came up with the phrase 'anthropic principle' (*anthropos* is the Greek word for 'human') to define the theory that the entire universe is fine-tuned to sustain intelligent life, and in particular human life, on our planet. His British counterpart John Polkinghorne agreed: 'We live in a universe whose constitution is precisely adjusted to the narrow limits which alone make it capable of being our home.'

Why should this be the case? Is the human race nothing more than one ingredient in a universal collection of gigantic flukes? Modern physics combines with biology to suggest that our amazingly ordered universe has been specifically and purposefully designed with humankind in mind. This ties in with our restless search for meaning, and the British mathematician and philosopher of science John Lennox cuts to the chase and makes this link between the ordered vastness of the universe and the significance of our lives: 'The starry heavens show the glory of God, yes; but they are not made in God's image. *You are.* That makes you unique. It gives you incalculable value. The galaxies are unimaginably large compared with you. However, you know that they exist, but they don't know that you exist. You are more significant, therefore than a galaxy. Size is not necessarily a reliable measure of value, as any woman can tell you as she looks at the diamonds on her finger and compares them with lumps of coal.'

Not only do these cosmic clues point to the intelligent and purposeful design of the universe and everything in it, there is also convincing evidence much closer to hand. We will take two chapters to lay this out as we look at some of the features that define us as human beings.

BODY LANGUAGE

The first piece of evidence is *our physical make-up*. In total, a human body has trillions of cells, with more than 100 different types, and according to the American chemist, biochemist and educator Linus Pauling a single cell is 'more complex than New York City.' On the BBC Radio 4 programme *Start the Week*, the British geneticist Alison Woollard was asked how these trillions of cells knew exactly what to do. She replied, 'This is a question that has vexed biologists for so long. We have about forty trillion cells in the average human body, and all of these cells do different things. So our heart cells do different things from our skin cells, for example. So cells must know what to do. And we know that cells know what to do because of the proteins they produce, and that they produce proteins because of the DNA sequence that they have inside all of our cells. But the real conundrum is the fact that all of our cells contain exactly the same DNA, the same genome. So how is it that cells can interpret this information in different ways, in order for cells to do the right thing at the right time and in the right place?' She was unable to answer her question, but surely interpreting information and doing 'the right thing at the right time' suggests intelligent and meaningful creation?

Within its trillions of cells, a human body has some seven billion billion atoms arranged in a specific and unique way. Those atoms are strings of genes that form genomes, and each person has over 20,000 protein-coding genes in the double helix structures that form DNA. Is this a biological accident or the product of natural forces that have no purpose—or does it confirm the Bible's claim in Genesis 1:27 that God created man? The American C. Everett Koop, who was widely regarded as the most influential Surgeon General in American history, made it clear where he stood on the issue: 'If I didn't believe that I had a God who was solid and dependable, a God who makes no mistakes, I couldn't continue what I'm doing. I never operate without having a sub-conscious feeling that there's no way this extraordinarily complicated mechanism known as the human body just happened to come up from slime and ooze ... When I make an incision with my scalpel, I see organs of such intricacy that there simply hasn't been enough time for natural evolutionary processes to have developed them.' A Boeing 747 airliner has over six million separate parts, and the technicians making and maintaining it know how every one of them works—but does this mean that the American aviation pioneer William Boeing, the founder of The Boeing Company, never existed? No scientific explanation of our body parts gives us a sufficient reason for their existence.

## THE SENSE OF SELF

Secondly, *we are both conscious and self-conscious.* Nobody can sensibly deny this, and the fact that we can find no natural way to explain it opens the door to there being a supernatural one, one that would in turn point to human life having unique meaning. The Polish-born British mathematician and biologist Jacob Bronowski claimed that 'living matter is not different in kind from dead matter,' and that 'man is part of nature, in the same sense that a stone is, or a cactus, or a camel,' but our self-consciousness proves the opposite. After all, if a camel could say, 'I am a camel,' it would no longer be a camel. If we are nothing but biological machines, how can we claim that anything we do has meaning? Yet we assume meaning in virtually everything we do. We make choices, we have friends, we enjoy things, we marry, we make love, we share ideas, impressions and possessions, we care for those in need, we give to charitable causes, we value truth, justice, friendship, compassion and sympathy.

A machine can do none of these things. Nor can any other living species. C. Everett Koop says that we are distinct from all other creatures in the world in that, 'We are able to know what is around us; the subject can know the object.' C. S. Lewis drives the point home: 'One of the things that distinguishes man from the other animals is that he wants to know things, wants to find out what reality is like, simply for the sake of knowing.' As human beings we are uniquely curious about the meaning of life and of our place in the world.

A CUT ABOVE

Thirdly, *we have a deep-rooted conviction that as human beings we have unique dignity*. We know instinctively that we are more than biological accidents. Even the strongly atheistic *Second Humanist Manifesto* speaks of 'the preciousness and dignity of the individual.'

Our sense of dignity is so ingrained that it extends even to the human body after death. In 2014 the Paralympian athlete Oscar Pistorius stood trial in South Africa for the murder of his girlfriend Reeva Steenkamp. When Gert Saayman, the pathologist who carried out the post-mortem examination on the victim, went to the witness stand he asked that, because of the graphic nature of the evidence he was about to give, all live broadcasts of the trial be switched off to protect 'the dignity of the deceased.' The judge agreed.

When terrorists demolished the twin towers of New York's World Trade Centre on 11 September 2001, only eighteen of the 2,753 victims were rescued alive. Yet so profound is our sense of human dignity that over the next thirteen years the city's Medical Examiner's Office, using ground-breaking forensic techniques, successfully identified 21,906 fragments of human remains (some less than one inch long) and returned them to the families of those concerned.

Peter Atkins claims that the human race is 'just a bit of slime on a planet,' but not even he lives as if this is true, and his atheism comes unstuck at this point. The atheist claims that life begins as an accident and will end in annihilation, yet he never lives as if his life means nothing. If human beings are essentially no different than other creatures, how can we claim to have any more value—or rights—than porcupines, pigs or pilchards?

Believing in the creation of the human race by God would explain our unique sense of dignity, and the Bible's fundamental statement on the subject is crystal clear: 'So God created man in his own image, in the image of God he created him; male and female he created them.' Being created 'in the image of God' has nothing to do with size, weight, shape or any other physical characteristics, as 'God is spirit' and has no physical or material properties. It means that we were created with personality, with powers of thought, feeling and will that go far beyond the brute instincts of other creatures. It also means that we are meant to relate to God in a way that is not true of any other living thing on the planet, and to know, appreciate, enjoy and worship him. This is what sets us apart from all other life forms and gives us a coherent reason for believing that a human being has more value than a virus.

## MIND MATTERS

Fourthly, *we are rational.* Richard Dawkins said, 'My brain is just a lump of meat,' but that hardly matches what we find. We not only think, but can think sensibly, using logic to assess theories, possibilities and suggestions. We can accumulate facts, and remember and evaluate vast amounts of information on an endless variety of subjects. We can process data, develop ideas, exercise our imagination and make rational decisions. We use verbal language to express our feelings, ideas, suggestions and conclusions. We can develop theories and concepts, and use technology to transform our lifestyles, and we have developed mathematical language to discuss issues ranging from the nature of the universe to statistics useful in daily life.

If our thoughts are the result of nothing more than the laws of physics shuffling atoms around in our brains, why should we believe that anything they produce is true or has any sensible meaning? How can we gain accurate knowledge about anything? How can we give our thoughts any moral, ethical or spiritual value? Why is thinking about anything of any more significance than a leaf falling from a tree? No normal person acts on the assumption that there is no meaning to what their mind is telling them.

## THE FORGOTTEN FACTOR

Fifthly, *we have an aesthetic dimension,* an important pointer that is often ignored or underestimated. Beauty is one of three fundamental values (truth and goodness are the other two) by which we judge the worth or value of things we see or hear. In doing this we take notice of such things as form, texture, colour, order or design—for example in nature, works of art, music and poetry. We are endlessly creative in developing new ways of expressing these. We can compose and enjoy so many things in literature and elsewhere. We can appreciate beauty in things we see, hear, smell, touch and taste.

The British molecular biologist Denis Alexander is right to claim, 'If the universe has no ultimate purpose, as atheism suggests, then the universal experience of being moved by works of great music or by other great acts of human creativity is difficult to explain.'

The British philosopher C. E. M. Joad, who abandoned his atheism late in life, wrote that goodness, truth and beauty are not just 'pieces of cosmic furniture lying about, as it were, in the universe without explanation, coherence or connection, but are revelations of a unity that underlies them,' and then added that they are 'the ways in which God reveals himself to man.' This reflects the Bible's teaching that in the wonders of the natural world God is pointing us to himself; it speaks in Psalm 27:4 of 'the beauty of the Lord.' In recognizing beauty we are responding as we should to who God is, and to what he has created (or enabled us to design, using materials he has supplied). Our recognition of beauty points to our having a meaning that goes far beyond our personal preferences.

# 7

# THE CLINCHERS

On one occasion the great artist Picasso was looking at the dust dancing in a ray of sunlight that slanted in through a high window. He commented, 'Nobody has any real importance to me. As far as I'm concerned, other people are like those little grains of dust floating in the sunlight. It takes only a push of the broom and out they go.' He was wrong, because nobody is insignificant. In the last chapter we looked at five reasons for believing that our lives have meaning and purpose. In this chapter we will look at two others that clinch the case.

## THE MORAL MAZE

*The first is that we have a moral dimension.* When C. S. Lewis wrote, 'Human beings, all over the earth, have this curious idea that they ought to behave in a certain way, and cannot get rid of it' he hit a hugely important nail on the head. Even if we try to play down what he says, we find ourselves behaving as if it is true. People may disagree on how they rate things on a moral scale, but we all have an inherent sense of right and wrong, something that separates us from every other species on the planet.

Other creatures are driven only by instinct, as when preying on other species, protecting their territory, fighting for food, or competing for mating partners. None of these brings a sense of identity into play, nor do they have any moral dimension. Is there any other species that asks where it came from, what it is and where it is going? Do sheep or snakes ever have an identity crisis or a concern about their long-term future? Does any other species have a moral dimension? Do dogs feel pangs of conscience when they foul pavements? Do cats ever repent for killing mice? As the British theologian Rod Garner points out, 'Rats, after all, as far as we know, show no particular enthusiasm for moral issues and questions of meaning; and chimpanzees, delightful though they are, are not normally to be seen on our streets collecting money for impoverished chimpanzees they will never meet.'

When Voldemort, the anti-hero in the J. K. Rowling's Harry Potter series, says, 'There is no such thing as good and evil. There is only power,' we know that he is talking nonsense. Everybody lives as if moral laws exist. Whenever we criticize what other people do, we are acknowledging that we are all subject to moral laws. What is more, morality is not a subject we can just discuss and leave it at that. It is something that affects our lives on a daily basis, and in our relationships with each other it is closely tied in to our dignity as human beings, regardless of our age or physical condition. As the Russian novelist and historian Aleksandr Solzhenitsyn put it, 'The line dividing good and evil cuts through the heart of every human being.' If there is no single, objective moral authority, we are all free to make up our own. But this would mean that if people disagree with each other about a particular moral issue, nobody could say that another person's opinions are wrong. If moral judgements are no more than personal opinions, we are like ships without rudders.

The fact that people have different opinions about whether something is right or wrong is not proof that there is no ultimate standard; in fact, it is exactly the opposite, and shows that we are all subject to one. There is a huge difference between preferences and principles, and nobody whose daughter is raped, whose car is stolen, or who in some other way suffers as the result of someone else's behaviour would settle for the first. A young man arguing strongly in favour of free sex soon back-pedalled when the philosopher Francis Schaeffer asked him for the name and telephone number of his live-in girlfriend!

ATOMS TO ETHICS?

Where does our sense of right and wrong come from? Richard Dawkins admits that 'as a biologist I haven't a very well worked-out story where that comes from.' Elsewhere, he is forced to concede. 'Much as we might wish to believe otherwise, universal love and the welfare of the species are concepts that simply do not make evolutionary sense.' How could they? If we trace the evolutionary idea from Darwin's 'warm little pond' to the unexplained appearance of life, then to life forms becoming more and more complex, then through amphibians to reptiles, birds, four-legged animals and eventually humans, at what point do accidental accumulations of atoms develop ethics, or molecules get ideas about morality? No scientific theory can explain it. John Lennox uses one of his favourite illustrations to make the point about the failure of science to define morality: 'Science can tell you that if you add strychnine to someone's drink it will kill them. But science cannot tell you whether it is morally right or wrong to put strychnine into your grandmother's tea so that you can get your hands on her property.'

When I was addressing a meeting in Oxford an atheist shouted at me, 'Morality is relative,' yet less than twenty-four hours earlier a Korean student at Virginia Polytechnic Institute and State University had killed thirty-two people and wounded twenty-five others in what was then the deadliest shooting incident by a single gunman in United States history. Was what he did relatively evil or absolutely evil? In May 2014 two teenage girls in the Indian village of Katra

Sadatganj, about 150 miles east of Delhi, were gang raped then hanged to death on a mango tree. They belonged to the Maurya caste, one of the lowest in the country. With no lavatory in their home, they had gone into a field to relieve themselves when they were apparently attacked, violated and murdered. The story went viral on the internet, and all around the world political leaders and others spoke of their disgust at this outrage. Nobody suggested it was relative.

We can no more do away with a moral law than we can do away with the law of gravity. If there is no such thing as a moral law we are free of any moral obligation—but so is everybody else, which means that we can have no complaint when anyone causes us pain, loss, harm or grief of any kind. If this were true it would lead to complete chaos in society, with everybody pursuing their own ends regardless of how their behaviour affected others. We can go further. If such a moral law exists there must be a moral lawgiver. As it is impossible to find morality anywhere in the natural world, its source must lie outside of nature. When he was still an atheist, C. S. Lewis set out to disprove the existence of God on the basis of logical argument. However, he soon began to realize that if God were not involved there would be no explanation for why people could rely on their own moral judgements. His argument against God collapsed when he realized that morality was not subjective (based on personal feelings, tastes, opinions or preferences) but objective (something that is 'out there,' regardless of what we believe, think or feel). He eventually came to see that if God does not exist, we have a universe without purpose, morality without a fixed reference point, and humanity without any moral meaning or purpose.

In a world without God, what one animal does to another animal is morally irrelevant, whether the animals concerned have four legs, two legs, or none. A statement widely attributed to the Russian author Fyodor Dostoyevsky claims, 'If there is no God, then all things are permitted.' In a letter to his fellow author N. L. Ozmidov he wrote, 'Now assume that there is no God, or immortality of the soul. Now tell me, why should I live righteously and do good deeds, if I am to die entirely on earth?... And if that is so, why shouldn't I (as long as I can rely on my cleverness and agility to avoid being caught by the law) cut another man's throat, rob and steal?'

The Bible paints a very different picture. It says in Romans 2:15 that all human beings, even those without any knowledge of God's written commandments have his law 'written on their hearts.' Francis Collins says, 'After twenty-eight years as a believer, the Moral Law still stands out for me as the strongest signpost to God. More than that, it points to a God who cares about human beings, and a God who is infinitely good and holy.' Elsewhere, he writes, 'This moral law, which defies scientific explanation, is exactly what one might expect to find if one were searching for the existence of a personal God who sought relationship with mankind.'

## THE GOD-SHAPED GAP

*The second and clearest of these powerful pointers is that we have a spiritual dimension.* No group of humans we have been able to trace in all of history seems to have been without religious belief of some kind, and this has always marked humanity out from the rest of creation. There is no evidence of religion in any other creatures—not even the praying mantis prays! If the human race had evolved from 'lower' forms of life, we should expect to find the earliest traceable humans in history without any signs of religious belief. Yet this is not the case, and as the American scholar Samuel Zwemer found, 'Religion is as old as the oldest record and is universal among the most primitive tribes today.' Some estimates say there are as many as 4,200 religious belief systems in the world today. In *The Encyclopaedia of Religion and Ethics*, the General Index alone runs to 660 pages. Countless people who might not claim to be religious regularly read their horoscopes to check their star signs, while others turn to Ouija boards, black magic, astrologers, mediums, palm readers and other occult practitioners in their attempts to reach into the spirit world.

Yet for all the religious ideas that humanity has held, the concept of there being just one true God has been by far the most persistent, in spite of it being relentlessly attacked by those determined to stamp it out. In the twentieth century alone, Marxist-Leninist Communism declared total warfare against it and the revolutionary leader Vladimir Lenin declared, 'Every religious idea, every idea of God, every flirtation with the idea of God, is unutterable vileness.' Persistent propaganda, brainwashing, imprisonment, torture and execution were all used in a vicious crusade against all believers in God. During the Cultural Revolution in China, beginning in 1966, the atheist dictator Mao Zedong had his opponents killed at the rate of 2,000 a month. Between 1975 and 1979 the Khmer Rouge movement, under its atheist leader Pol Pot, slaughtered over 1,500,000 Cambodians out of a population of about 8,000,000 in the notorious 'killing fields.' Since then, godless regimes in many countries have repressed, bullied, tortured and killed countless people for no other reason than that they believed in God.

More people were killed because of their faith in God during the twentieth century than in the previous nineteen centuries put together, yet the American author Paul Johnson has pointed out this remarkable fact: 'The most extraordinary thing about the twentieth century was the failure of God to die. The collapse of mass religious belief, especially among the educated and prosperous, had been widely and confidently predicted. It did not take place. Somehow, God survived, flourished even. At the end of the twentieth century the idea of a personal, living God is as lively and real as ever in the minds and hearts of countless millions of men and women throughout our planet.'

While all other creatures seem satisfied when their basic physical needs have been met, human beings are not. As the French mathematician, philosopher and scientist Blaise Pascal put it, 'There is a God-shaped vacuum in the heart of every person that cannot be filled by any created thing, but only by God, the Creator.'

The Bible's explanation in Genesis 1:27 for this is the perfectly straightforward statement we saw in the last chapter: 'So God created man in his own image, in the image of God he created him; male and female he created them.' The human race was not created *with* the image of God but '*in* the image of God'. This does not mean that each person is a miniature God, but being created in his image is what marks human beings out from all other creatures. Without being made divine, we were created with qualities which enable us to enjoy a living relationship with our Maker.

This not only helps to explain our unique dignity, it also gives us a moral framework for our lives. As his representatives, we are stewards of all that God has given to us. He has made us responsible for carrying out his wishes, including taking care of the planet on which he has placed us —and doing so in a way that reflects his holiness, beauty and goodness in our lives. It is impossible to imagine how our lives could have greater meaning or purpose.

Yet all our searching for life's meaning is framed by one simple truth that none of us can avoid and that puts all of our thinking about life in context. We will turn to that now.

# 8

## AND THEN...

The Oscar-winning film *Schindler's List* tells how a German businessman Oskar Schindler, although a member of the Nazi Party, became concerned at the appalling persecution of Jews in Poland during the Holocaust in the Second World War. He used many different schemes to employ Jews in his factory, helping to save the lives of over a thousand people. At one point in the film, when trying to help friends cope with the random slaughter of their fellow Jews, he delivers this chilling line: *'People die. That's life.'*

Life can be exciting, enjoyable, satisfying and rewarding. It can also be dull, miserable, unpleasant and heartbreaking. Most lives are a mixture of these, but they have one thing in common—they come to an end. Whether the end closes in slowly after a long illness or disease, or comes abruptly by accident or in some other way, at one moment the person concerned is alive, and a nanosecond later they are dead. The brain stops functioning, the heart stops beating, the rest of the vital organs shut down, and a character becomes a corpse.

It may seem strange, in a book about the meaning of life, to devote a whole chapter to death, yet what we call 'living' could just as accurately be called 'dying,' as death stalks our every step from the cradle to the grave. What we think about death has a profound effect on how we live, and on whether we see life as having any meaning or purpose. Blaise Pascal said he had learned to define life backwards and live it forwards. By this he meant that he began by defining death— then lived accordingly. This was good thinking on his part. When we know a destination we aim to get there in the right way. If we ignore the issue of death we will never get a clear picture of whether life has any meaning and purpose. In the context of this book, the link between life and death is obvious. For example, as the American scholar J. Ligon Duncan III says, 'If you believe that there is no God, and that this world evolved from a primitive protein in the explosion of some primary particle, then death is literally meaningless.'

One approach to the subject of death is to try to ignore it. It is said that King Louis XV of France told his servants never to mention the word 'death' in his presence. Today, the word 'died' is often replaced by 'passed away,' 'moved on,' 'no longer with us' or 'gone to pastures new.' To avoid getting too close to the subject, people often use trivial terms and speak of someone having 'kicked the bucket,' 'snuffed it,' 'bitten the dust' or 'popped their clogs' or are later said to be 'pushing up daisies' or to be 'six feet under.'

Others try to fight it off with humour. The British journalist Kate Saunders told readers of *The Daily Telegraph*, 'If I am cremated, I don't intend to sit in a jar on the mantelpiece depressing my husband. What if my urn got broken? I have therefore decided that my ashes will be scattered in my favourite place—up the noses of certain former employers.' The family of New Orleans resident Miriam Burbank followed her instructions and at her funeral service propped her body up sitting at a table, wearing sunglasses and carrying a glass of wine in one hand and a menthol cigarette in the other. The funeral director said that this kind of thing was not unusual and that his company prided itself in putting the 'fun' into 'funeral.' Statements like this may be amusing to some people, but they do nothing to dispel death's reality or meaning.

## NOWHERE TO GO?

The American author Ernest Hemingway claimed, 'Life is just a dirty trick, a short journey from nothingness to nothingness. There is no remedy for anything in life. Man's destiny in the universe is like a colony of ants on a burning log.' He committed suicide three weeks short of what would have been his sixty-second birthday. Mourners at the funeral in 2010 of Malcolm McLaren, manager of the British rock band Sex Pistols, travelled in a bus with the destination sign 'Nowhere.' But the idea that death ends everything robs life of any semblance of meaning; as Jean-Paul Sartre saw it, 'Man is a useless passion. It is meaningless that we live, and it is meaningless that we die.'

## WHO'S AFRAID?

Many more people than would be prepared to admit it are afraid of death. J. K. Rowling says, 'My books are largely about death. They open with the death of Harry's parents. There is Voldemort's obsession with conquering death and his quest for immortality at any price, the goal for anyone with magic... I so understand why Voldemort wants to conquer death. We're all frightened of it.' The Bible in Hebrews 2:15 is not exaggerating when it speaks of those who 'through fear of death were subject to lifelong slavery' and of people being 'brought to the king of terrors' (Job 18:14) and it is easy to understand why.

*There is fear of the unknown.* We may have been present when someone has died, but none of us has ever experienced death for ourselves—and we have an inbuilt dread of the unknown. Speaking at a Ways with Words Festival, the British broadcaster and author Melvyn Bragg told his audience, 'We are reaching into the unknown. We are going somewhere and we don't know what the end is.'

*There is fear of the pain, disability or disintegration that might precede death.* Nobody can look forward to weeks, months or years of suffering, knowing that things can only get worse. The British clergyman and poet G. S. Studdert Kennedy, who as an army chaplain ministered to injured and dying soldiers during the First World War, said that anyone who was not disturbed by the problem of pain was suffering from hardness of the heart or softening of the brain.

*There is fear that old age will drain life of its meaning.* The British journalist and television presenter Joan Bakewell writes of many old people, 'They get lonely, they can get depressed. Let's face it, at my age [she was 80 at the time] almost everyone is left with a smattering of disappointed hopes and no time to do anything about it. Too late to climb that mountain, build that dream house. But too late also to make up for broken relationships, damaged bonds, neglected friends… Ageing deprives us of the sense of purpose that drives us forward through our earlier, and indeed middle years. Suddenly, we aren't going anywhere, aiming for anything specific… the golden years of flourishing are gone for ever.'

*There is fear that death will end a life that never gave us what we were looking for.* When he was at the peak of his career, the British actor and comedian Kenneth Williams agonized over whether his life would count for anything and said, 'The madness screaming up inside me. So many awful thoughts— this terrible sense of doom hanging over me. I wonder if anyone will ever know about the emptiness of my life. I wonder if anyone will ever stand in a room that I have lived in and touch the things that were once a part of my life and wonder about me?… Now I am thinking all the while of death in some shape or another. Every day is something to be got through. All the recipes of the past are no longer valid. I've spent all my life in the mind. I have entered into nothing.'

*There is fear that death will leave us not only with unfinished business, but with unfinished pleasure.* Included among the many golf-related books I have is one titled *1001 Golf Holes You Must Play Before You Die.* I drool and dream every time I open it, but I know that although I have played hundreds of courses all around the world I will never play more than a tiny percentage of those listed in the book. For over forty years I have lived within fifteen miles of the centre of London, judged by many to be the greatest city in the world and bursting at the seams with historic buildings and objects, but I know that I will never see more than a tiny percentage of them. Yet what if I was to play every one of the golf holes mentioned in the book and see every historic building and object London has to offer? Would doing so add any meaning to my life? The certainty of death should tell us that life is meant to be more than satisfaction in the here and now. We invest so much time, energy, money, enthusiasm and effort into the business and pleasures of life, all the time knowing with nagging certainty that everything we accumulate, value or enjoy will one day be taken away.

*There is fear of meeting God.* Many who never give more than a passing thought to this may do so if they attend a funeral. The words of the service may make them think that meeting God is at least a possibility, and an uncomfortable one at that. The British racing driver Stirling Moss, winner of sixteen Grand Prix events and rated the greatest driver never to win the World Championship, was noted for his great courage on the racetrack, yet he told a newspaper reporter, 'I am frightened of death. I know it means going to meet my Maker, and one shouldn't be afraid of that. But I am.'

### THE FACTS OF DEATH

Much of this chapter has been taken up with people's comments or opinions. We can close it with some straightforward facts about death that will help us to get our question about the meaning of life into perspective.

*Life is brief.* The British clergyman Henry Twells once

wrote a poem he called 'Time's Paces' and which is fixed to the front face of the clock case in the north transept of Chester Cathedral. The opening lines run like this:

> *When as a child I laughed and wept,*
> *Time crept.*
> *When as a youth I dreamt and talked,*
> *Time walked.*
> *When I became a full-grown man,*
> *Time ran.*
> *When older still I daily grew,*
> *Time flew.*
> *Soon I shall find in travelling on—*
> *Time gone.*

The Bible in James 4:14 asks and answers a question about life like this: 'What is your life? For you are a mist that appears for a little time and then vanishes.'

*Death can come at any time, by design, disease, decay or disaster.* Death comes to young and old, rich and poor, good and bad, educated and otherwise, king and commoner. The dynamic young businessman, the glamorous actress, the outstanding athlete, the brilliant scientist, the popular television personality and the powerful politician are all in the same boat—none can avoid the moment when death will bring all their power, possessions and achievements to nothing.

*We still exist after death.* Science tells us that no part of the universe is self-created and that nothing can ever be completely wiped out. That includes our bodies. They may not remain in the same state, or function in the same way, but they will always exist. If you beat up an egg to make an omelette the egg still exists, even though there is no way in which a chicken can be hatched from it. The substance of the egg-turned-omelette will never be annihilated, not even after you have eaten it. This law operates everywhere in nature.

The Bible teems with the fundamental truth that *death does not mean annihilation, but separation.* Death does not put an end to a person's existence. The human spirit does not depend on the body for its existence and continues to be alive after the body has ceased to function. This is hugely important when we search for the meaning and purpose of life. The British author H. G. Wells wrote, 'If there is no afterlife, then life is just a sick joke, braying across the centuries.' Francis Schaeffer wrote, 'All men... have a deep longing for significance, a longing for meaning... No man... is content to look at himself as a finally meaningless machine which can and will be discarded totally and for ever.' Unless there is life beyond the grave, all our concerns about values such as truth, justice, love and meaning are a classic case of rearranging the deckchairs on the Titanic.

*Death is followed by judgement.* Bertrand Russell said, 'I believe that when I die I shall rot, and nothing of my ego will survive,' but this was wishful thinking, as the Bible warns us that 'it is appointed for man to die once, and after that comes judgement' (Hebrews 9:27) when 'each of us will give an account of himself to God' (Romans 14:12). God is not only a God of love, but he is also a God of perfect justice, and we need to be aware of both. As an article in *Punch* put it, 'You can't just have the bits of God you like and leave out the stuff you're not so happy with.'

We have a built-in instinct for justice. We make much of the idea that justice should be done, and be seen to be done— and we would want to press for it to be done if someone committed a crime against us. As God is 'righteous in all his ways' (Psalm 145:17), a wise person will want to think very carefully about the day when they will appear before him and give account of their life. Try as we might to avoid even thinking about it, final judgement is inescapable. Only when we know how to die will we know how to live—but how can we do this?

When the British fantasy writer Terry Pratchett died in 2015 at the age of sixty-six after an eight-year battle with Alzheimer's disease, thousands of fans felt cheated and signed a petition calling on Death to hand him back. It never did. If we could find one person in human history who faced life's pressures and problems and came through all of them unscathed, who knew with absolute certainty why he was born and what the meaning of life is, then not only died but overcame death, we would finally be on track to answer the question with which we started this book.

One man did…

# 9

# THE EXCEPTION

*a* first look at the early part of his life makes him look like the last person who could show us that life has any meaning, or explain what that meaning is.

He was born in some kind of outhouse about 2,000 years ago, but we are not sure of the year, can only guess at the month, and have no clue as to the exact date. He grew up in a town with such a poor reputation that anyone giving it as their address when applying for a job might not even get an interview. We know very little about him during his childhood. Unmarried, he left home when he was about thirty years old, and began travelling the country, with no fixed abode, fulfilling what he said was his life's mission.

In the course of this, he never did any of the things that normally help to push people up the social ladder. He was never elected to public office, or to lead any social group of his peers. He had no financial backing, never earned a salary and never issued any publicity. He never wrote a book, painted a picture, or composed any poetry or music. He never raised an army, or led a rebellion, and only once travelled outside of his tiny native country. He had no formal education and never owned any property, and at one point even had to borrow a coin to illustrate a point he was making.

Early on in his career he became the target for all kinds of criticism, especially from those in the religious establishment, whose noses he put severely out of joint by his teaching about the meaning of life and how it should be lived. They accused him of deceiving people and encouraging them to break long-established laws. When he began to attract huge crowds, the authorities decided that there was only one way to stop him, and that was to have him put to death. They had him arrested and put on trial before both religious and civil authorities. The trials were held in three stages over a period of nine hours, beginning late at night. Legal rules were swept aside in the prosecution's determination to see the prisoner sentenced and punished as quickly as possible.

Although witnesses at his first religious trial lied through their teeth, the presiding officer accepted the charges brought against him and agreed that he should be executed. Early the following morning the prosecutors sent him for trial before the Roman governor, and switched the charge to treason. When the governor told them the accused was not guilty of this, they hauled the prisoner before the Romans' client king who happened to be in the city at the time. This mockery of a trial turned out to be a non-event, as the prisoner refused to say a word. He was then sent back to the governor, who repeated his verdict of Not Guilty, but by now a crowd had been whipped up into a storm of hatred and demanded that the prisoner be executed by crucifixion. This was the most humiliating and agonizing form of capital punishment then in use, but to avoid a riot the governor finally caved in and literally washed his hands of the case. Soldiers then stripped the prisoner naked, spat on him, dressed him up to look like a king, kneeled before him in mock worship, and led him away to be executed in public.

While the victim was hanging on a huge cross, pinned there by nails driven through his hands and feet, he was mocked and jeered at by his persecutors and passers-by. Three horrific hours later he died. The bodies of crucified criminals remained the property of the Romans, but that evening one of the victim's friends asked for the body and was given permission to remove it. He then placed it in a tomb (a cave cut out of a nearby cliff) which he had bought for his own burial, and closed the entrance to it with a huge rock.

If there was nothing else to go on, it would seem farcical to put this man forward, out of the sixty billion people in human history, as the only person who can tell us whether life has any meaning, or show us what that meaning is. All we have to go on is the blood-stained corpse of someone who seems to have been a born loser. As the American historian Kenneth Scott Latourette wrote, 'So far as the casual spectator late on the afternoon of the execution could have seen, [his] work had ended in failure.' But the story does not end there...

## DAY 3

Because the deceased had attracted so much attention over the previous three years, the Roman governor had ordered the rock closing the entrance to the cave to be secured with his official seal (breaking it would result in the death penalty). For added security he put a squad of soldiers in place to guard it. Yet history records that within three days one staggering fact triggered everything that was to follow: *the body had gone.* The British academic Sir Norman Anderson one-time Director of the Institute of Advanced Legal Studies at the University of London, claimed, 'There was no point in arguing about the empty tomb. Everyone, friend and opponent, knew that it was empty. The only questions worth arguing about were why it was empty and what its emptiness proved.'

A few weeks later an even greater bombshell hit the city— his followers took to the streets with the sensational announcement that the man who had been persecuted, brutalized, executed and buried had come back to life and had met with them several times.

*His name was Jesus, sometimes known as Jesus of Nazareth (to link him with his home town) and nothing is more important in our search for the meaning of life than his resurrection from the dead.*

It is not difficult to imagine that the social media of the time (rumour and gossip) went into overdrive. Bloggers would have had a field day, and there have been more conspiracy theories on the issue than surrounded the assassination of US President John F. Kennedy in 1963. Here are some of them.

*The Roman authorities removed the body.* They obviously had the opportunity, but what motive would they have had? When his followers claimed to have seen him alive again, the Romans could immediately have produced the dead body and proved that his followers were deluded fools.

*His persecutors removed it.* It is impossible to imagine why they would have done this—and one other thing makes the idea ridiculous. In the course of his teaching, Jesus had not only forecast that he would be persecuted, condemned and executed, but that he would rise from the dead after three days. When his followers claimed that he had done so, all his persecutors had to do was to produce the body after *four* days and those claims would have collapsed.

*His followers stole the body.* But why? Not only had the body been safely laid in the tomb of a close friend, but they had already locked themselves into a safe house for fear that they might be next on the religious authorities' hit list. How (and why) did this handful of terrified mourners pluck up the courage to tackle an armed guard merely to lay hold of a corpse?

*Jesus never actually died.* This is the most absurd theory of all. It says that while hanging on the cross Jesus went into a coma and was still in it when he was placed into the tomb. It took over 1,800 years for this idea to come to life, but it never gets to its feet. Before the body was removed for burial the execution squad certified that Jesus was dead. If he was merely comatose, why did none of the friends who carried him to the tomb notice that he was still breathing? After being buried, how did he recover, wriggle his way out of tightly-wound grave-clothes, push aside the great rock closing off the cave, break the governor's seal and overpower the security guards? One more thing: when his friends went to the tomb a few days later they 'saw the linen cloths lying there, and the face cloth, which had been on Jesus' head, not lying with the linen cloths but folded up in a place by itself' (John 20:6-7). Assuming that he had managed to extricate himself from these wrappings, why would he leave them behind (taking the trouble to fold up the head covering neatly) before walking away when he had nothing else to wear? Of all the alternative theories trying to explain away what happened, this is surely the most ridiculous?

EVIDENCE

It is now about 2,000 years since Jesus was executed and buried, yet nobody has been able to come up with a good explanation to replace the Bible's record of why his grave was empty, unless he rose from the dead. On the other hand, there is a lot of powerful evidence to prove that he did.

*Hundreds of people claimed that they had seen him.* Six independent witnesses record eleven separate appearances over a period of forty days. These were not hallucinations, nor had they seen a ghost. Some of them had talked with him, touched him, and even shared several meals with him. On one occasion he appeared to over 500 people at once. When recording this some time later, one New Testament writer said that most of them were still alive, so could have been asked to describe exactly what had happened. What possible motive could they have had for making these claims? Why would they have risked persecution (or worse) by openly identifying themselves with someone the authorities had hounded to death as Public Enemy Number One?

*His followers were transformed.* As we saw earlier, immediately after his death they hid behind locked doors, terrified of being persecuted. Yet soon afterwards they came out of hiding, took to the streets, and staked their lives by insisting on one thing: *Jesus was alive.* They were persecuted, arrested, prosecuted, punished and threatened with execution, but nothing could stop them. Why expose themselves to all of this if they knew they were lying? The American philosopher Peter Kreeft makes the point well: 'Liars always lie for selfish reasons. If they lied, what was their motive; what did they get out of it? What they got out of it was misunderstanding, rejection, persecution and martyrdom. Hardly a list of perks!' People are sometimes willing to suffer and die for something they believe to be true, *but never for something they know to be false.* Sir Norman Anderson went so far as to say that the transformed lives of Jesus' early followers was 'far and away the strongest circumstantial evidence of the resurrection.'

*The Christian church came into existence.* Those few first believers were the founders of what has since become the largest religious body the world has ever known. In spite of greater opposition, more persecution, and more martyrs than any other grouping in history it has continued to grow for 2,000 years and today has billions of members living in every country in the world—and its foundation was the resurrection of Jesus.

Over the centuries the Christian church has rightly been criticized for some of the appalling things done in its name, but these have never reflected the character or the teaching of its founder. Forged currency gives us no reason for rejecting the real thing. The Christian church has been the greatest force for good the world has ever known. Its influence in the field of education, in meeting the needs of the sick, the disadvantaged, the homeless, widows and orphans, and the victims of war, violence and 'man's inhumanity to man' is without parallel—and it owes its very existence to one historical event: *the resurrection of Jesus from the dead.*

The American-born British lawyer and politician John Singleton Copley, was one of the greatest minds in British legal history, and was three times Lord High Chancellor of Great Britain. In a document found among his private papers after his death he delivered this powerful verdict: 'I know pretty well what evidence is; and I tell you, such evidence as that for the resurrection has never broken down yet.'

## IDENTITY

Jesus is the most controversial person in history. All his recorded words and actions have been analysed and debated by countless experts and others over the centuries. Yet the most contentious issue about him is not what he taught, but who he was, and one Bible statement in Romans 1:4 confirms this tremendous truth: he was *declared to be the Son of God in power … by his resurrection from the dead.'*

In the musical *Jesus Christ Superstar,* Mary Magdalene sings of Jesus, 'He's a man, he's just a man,' but this is at best a half-truth. Jesus was not only a man, he was also God in human flesh and form. In John Lennox's great phrase, 'God coded himself into humanity.' He was not mainly God and partly man, nor was he mainly man and partly God. Instead, he was both fully God and fully man, as fully human as if he was not divine, yet as fully divine as if he was not human. As the distinguished theologian J. I. Packer put it 'The Almighty appeared on earth as a helpless human baby, unable to do more than lie and stare and wriggle and make noises, needing to be fed and changed and taught to talk like any other child… The more you think about it, the more staggering it gets.'

This tells us that Jesus did not become the Son of God at his resurrection, nor even at his birth. He was the Son of God *before* he stepped into human history and became the son of his human mother. He had a birth, but no beginning. Instead, as he told a religious leader in John 3:13, he 'descended from heaven.'

## INDICATIONS

His resurrection from the dead was the most dramatic proof in the New Testament that Jesus is both God and man, but the quality of his life also speaks volumes. Although he was 'tempted as we are' he was absolutely faultless and 'without sin' (Hebrews 4:15). There is also the record of his amazing miracles, that included the healing of physical, mental and psychological disease, and even on at least three occasions, the raising of people from the dead. One New Testament writer in John 21:25 says of Jesus' miracles, 'Were every one of them to be written, I suppose that the world itself could not contain the books that would be written.' The French artist, illustrator and sculptor Paul Gustave Doré once lost his passport while travelling. At the next international border he explained his problem to an immigration official and assured him that he was who he claimed to be. The official handed him a piece of paper and a pencil and said, 'Prove it!' Doré quickly produced such a brilliant sketch that the official had all the evidence he needed. The things Jesus did prove who he was.

IMPLICATIONS

Everything we have seen in this chapter points to some important implications as far as our search for the meaning of life is concerned. These are all pinned to the fact that Jesus knew exactly why he came into the world.

*He came to show us what God is like.* The Bible tells us that 'no one has ever seen God,' yet in the same sentence we are told that Jesus 'has made him known' (John 1:18). In Jesus we see a human illustration of God's character, and he made this crystal clear time and again. When one of his closest followers asked him to show them the Father [God], as that would clinch their faith, Jesus replied, 'Whoever has seen me has seen the Father' (John 14:9). How could he lie about his identity if he never lied about anything? After being put under critical microscopes for 2,000 years, not a single fault has ever been found in him. *If he was not God, he was not even good; if he was not good he was not God.* There is no room for manoeuvre here.

*He came to do God's will and so fulfil his purposes.* He told people in John 6:38, 'I have come down from heaven, not to do my own will but the will of him who sent me.' This is what ultimately gave his life meaning. Everything he did was aimed at fulfilling God's purpose for his earthly life, and he did this so perfectly that he had no hesitation in saying, 'I always do the things that are pleasing to him' (John 8:29).

This still leaves us with the all-important question of how what one man did 2,000 years ago can have any relevance to our lives, and in particular how it can help us to find their intended meaning and purpose. The final two chapters will make the answer clear.

# 10

# THE SUBSTITUTE

*a* person's hope of finding whether life has any meaning depends entirely on their worldview—and everybody has one. Put at its very simplest, a worldview is how a person views the world. If you wear a pair of blue-tinted spectacles or sunglasses, everything you see will be affected by that colour, and a different-coloured tint will affect what you see in the same way. Your worldview is what you 'put on' (assume to be true) before you look at anything, whether it be the natural world, your relationship to it, or life as a whole, including your view as to whether it has any meaning or purpose.

The American author Teresa Turner Vining gives us a vivid example of what it means to have the wrong worldview. She tells of the time when, as a university student, the atheistic worldviews of her professors were adding to her growing doubts about having faith in God: *what if it was all a lie?* She records what happened when she returned to her apartment one day: 'Lying in bed surrounded by darkness, I tried to grasp the significance of it all. There is no God, I told myself. This life is all there is. No one really knows why we are here or how we got here. There is nothing more than self-centred, imperfect humanity in which to hope. There is no real meaning, no basis for knowing what is right and wrong. It doesn't matter what we do or how we live. There is no foundation, no right and wrong, no hope. *No!* something deep inside of me screamed. It could not be true. I couldn't believe that life was just a sick joke with humans and their capacity for love, appreciation of beauty, and need for meaning as the pitiful punch line. That went against all my experience as a human being. There had to be something more!… Something deep inside me seemed to testify that somehow "good" is better than "bad" and "love" is better than "hate," and that meant we must be something more than just a sum of atoms.'

This brings us to the very heart of what this book is all about. To put it as simply and directly as I can—*the meaning of your life is not about you!*

All of us were created by God and for God and will never see life in its right perspective until we accept this. The worldview that can point us to life's meaning and purpose is not one that cobbles together our own likes and dislikes, views and opinions, hopes and fears, pursuits and pleasures, possessions and positions. Nothing we have or do can fill the God-shaped vacuum we mentioned in Chapter 7. Health, possessions, wealth, popularity, pleasure or success may take our minds off it for a while, but they are no more than low-dose painkillers, and in the depths of our hearts we know that they do nothing to meet our greatest need. Life is not about what satisfies our feelings in the here and now. As C. S. Lewis explained, 'All that is not eternal is eternally out of date.'

Looking for a meaning to life without putting God at the centre of one's thinking is worse than looking for a needle in a haystack, as there is not even a haystack. If we were not created by God, and are just biological accidents made from bits of our ancestors, why should anything we do have any more meaning or significance than the activities of a mouse or a worm? If we were born by accident and are on our way to annihilation we can abandon any idea of life having ultimate meaning, and nothing we accumulate or pour into it will leave it anything other than empty and pointless. In that kind of search for meaning, Woody Allen says we create a fake world, one that 'in fact, means nothing at all when you step back. It's meaningless.' The Swiss psychiatrist and psychotherapist Carl Gustav Jung put it like this: 'Men cut themselves from the root of their being, from God, and then life turns empty, inane, meaningless, without purpose, so when God goes, goal goes, when goal goes, meaning goes, when meaning goes, value goes, and life turns empty in our hands.'

On the other hand, if we believe there is a God who made, understands and loves us, and has a purpose for our lives, our approach will be very different—and the Bible points us in that direction. It tells us that God is not only the creator and sustainer of the universe, but that he has set out his purpose for all of his creation. This includes rescuing us from the futile task of trying to find life's meaning and purpose while having the wrong worldview.

FACTS TO FACE

In our search for the meaning of life there are certain critical facts we need to face—and we must begin at the beginning. The Bible tells us that man was 'created after the likeness of God in true righteousness and holiness' (Ephesians 4:24). Our first parents not only had the right worldview, with God at the centre of their thinking, they were also obedient to all that God required of them, and as a result enjoyed a perfect relationship with him, with each other, and with all of nature. Then at some point things went disastrously wrong: 'Sin came into the world through one man, and death through sin' (Romans 5:12). The word 'sin' is not one we like being attached to us, and none of us appreciates being called a sinner, but this is mainly because we do not understand what the Bible means by sin. Simply put, it means anything—a thought, a word or an action—that is less than perfect and does not meet God's standard. If we grasp this, we should have no difficulty in accepting what the Bible says about us.

Early in human history, humanity rejected God's authority and believed they could determine right and wrong for themselves. From that moment, our relationship with God was wrecked, our innocence and free will were lost, our nature was corrupted, and our worldview was skewed, becoming self-centred instead of God-centred.

What is more, every generation since (including ours) inherits this fallen nature and all of its appalling consequences. These include being subject to God's righteous anger here and now, and doomed to experience it in much fuller measure after we die. The Bible is crystal clear that 'we will all stand before the judgement seat of God' (Romans 14:10) to whom 'each of us will give an account' (Romans 14:12). We will not then be annihilated, but as 'nothing unclean will ever enter [heaven]' (Revelation 21:27) Jesus warned us that all who are not right with God will be 'sentenced to hell' (Matthew 23:33), which he called a place of 'eternal punishment' (Matthew 25:46). This final judgement confirms that although we often complain about justice not being done in this world, we can be sure that there will be perfect and ultimate justice in the world to come.

## GOD STEPS IN

Now we can see the answer to the question we asked at the end of the previous chapter. We can begin to grasp the meaning of life when we realize that God has stepped in to rescue us from everything that follows on from having the wrong worldview. When Jesus was born, it was God himself coming into our broken world and providing a way by which we can have our worldview transformed, be brought into a living relationship with him, and begin living a God-centred life, one with the meaning and purpose he intended us to have. Jesus not only lived a perfect life, performed amazing miracles and gave uniquely brilliant teaching about the meaning of life, he did something that fulfilled his own purpose for coming into the world. The British author

Dorothy L. Sayers wrote a controversial radio drama on the life of Jesus called *The Man born to be King*, but the title was misleading. Jesus was not born to be king—he was already 'King of kings and Lord of lords' (Revelation 19:16) before he was born. He was not born to be king, *he was a king born to die*.

In 2006 a man in the United States broke the world record by having his 1000th body piercing. Asked why he had done this, he replied, 'I wanted to do something useful with my life'! This triviality is in stark contrast to the fact that Jesus came into the world to do something that was truly astonishing—he 'laid down his life for us' (1 John 3:16). Although he himself had no sin of any kind, Jesus took the place of sinners, and in his death on the cross suffered the penalty their sins deserved, becoming as accountable for them as if he had been responsible for them. In the Bible's words, Jesus died, 'the righteous for the unrighteous, that he might bring us to God' (1 Peter 3:18) and so restore our broken relationship with him.

No human sacrifice is sufficient to illustrate this, but an incident from the Second World War points us in the right direction. Ernest Gordon was a company commander with the 2nd Battalion, Argyll and Sutherland Highlanders, and served in several campaigns, including those in Burma and Singapore. He spent three years in a Japanese prisoner of war camp and in *Miracle on the River Kwai* he told this remarkable story. When the prisoners had finished a day's work a Japanese guard shouted that a shovel was missing, and demanded that whoever had stolen it must step forward to be punished. When nobody moved, he raised his rifle and screamed, 'All die! All die!' When he aimed it at the first prisoner in the line, a young soldier stepped forward and said, 'I did it.' The guard then beat him to death, finally crushing his head with the butt of his rifle. When the prisoners marched back to camp and the tools were counted it was found that none was missing. This is a stunning story of courage and sacrifice on behalf of others, yet it is still only a pale reflection of what Jesus did in bearing in his body and spirit the punishment that other people rightly deserve.

Why do such a thing? The Bible's only explanation, in Romans 5:8, is this—'*God shows his love for us* in that while we were still sinners, Christ died for us.' God does not love us because he finds us attractive or because we deserve his love. Exactly the opposite is the case; Jesus loved us by dying in our place 'while we were [his] enemies' (Romans 5:10). There is nothing in any other religion that remotely compares with this.

We can also know that Jesus paid sin's penalty in full because he rose from the dead on the third day, the clearest possible proof that even death had been defeated and 'no longer has dominion over him' (Romans 6:9). C. S. Lewis put it brilliantly: 'He has forced open a door that had been locked since the death of the first man. He has met, fought and beaten the King of Death. Everything is different because he has done so. This is the beginning of the new creation. A new chapter in cosmic history has opened.'

This amazing mission was not 'Plan B' on God's part. It was something planned 'before the foundation of the world' (1 Peter 1:20). In all of this, Jesus was not acting on a sudden impulse, or carrying out an idea that grew on him during his thirty or so years on earth. He made this clear when a few hours before his death he anticipated it by telling God, 'I glorified you on earth, having accomplished the work that you gave me to do' (John 17:4). This 'work' was dying in the place of sinners, and so paying the penalty for their sin. As he said just before his arrest and crucifixion, 'For this purpose I have come to this hour' (John 12:27).

In an amazing demonstration of divine love, Jesus came into the world to save us from the appalling fate we deserve. The final chapter explains what our response should be, and how the right one will lead us to find life's true meaning and purpose.

# 11

# THE ANSWER

*I*n this final chapter I want to write to you personally and directly as if we were alone and talking to each other face to face. This is not the usual way to end a book that has so far been written to a wider readership, but there are times when style is secondary, and this is one of them. Discovering whether your life has any meaning is crucially important, and I want to do everything I can to help you to do so.

## FIRST THINGS FIRST

The right way to begin is not by shaking together a cocktail of your own thoughts, ideas, preferences and circumstances, but by recognizing that *God's glory is the most important thing in the entire universe.* Everything the Bible says about this is summed up in four words: he is called 'the God of glory' (Acts 7:2). God's glory is nothing less than all that he is by nature. It is his awesome and infinite majesty, radiance, beauty and perfection. 'Absolutely' is one of the most overused words in the English language. No experience is absolutely delightful, no meal is absolutely perfect, no holiday is absolutely marvellous, and no person is absolutely wonderful, but when we describe God 'absolutely' is always the right word to use. He is absolutely sovereign; 'his kingdom rules over all' (Psalm 103:19). He is absolutely perfect; 'God is light, and in him is no darkness at all' (1 John 1:5). He is absolutely powerful; 'Surpassing power belongs to God' (2 Corinthians 4:7). He is absolutely loving; 'God is love' 1 John 4:16). He is absolutely just; 'All his works are right and his ways are just' (Daniel 4:37). Here are some of the ways in which the Bible says God reveals his glory:

'The heavens declare the glory of God, and the sky above proclaims his handiwork' (Psalm 19:1). In Chapter 5 we saw this as a cosmic clue that we are not accidental by-products of nature living on a tiny speck of dust lost in a universe without meaning.

'The whole earth is full of [God's] glory' (Isaiah 6:3)! In spite of being polluted by man's sin, our planet teems with dynamic, living evidence pointing to an intelligent Creator. The amazing complexity and elegance of the genetic code alone is sufficient to give Francis Collins 'a compelling demonstration of God's role in creating life.'

Jesus revealed God's glory when he came to earth over 2,000 years ago. One of the Bible's names for him is 'the Word,' and we are told in John 1:14, 'The Word became flesh and dwelt among us, and we have seen his glory, glory as of the only Son from the Father, full of grace and truth.' Jesus was God spelling himself out in a way that we could see and understand. As we study his life we see 'the light of the knowledge of the glory of God' (2 Corinthians 4:6). He revealed God's glory in his unique wisdom, his perfect holiness, his countless miracles, his faultless judgement, his amazing grace, his voluntary death in our place and his resurrection from the dead.

## REALITY CHECK

Now comes the challenging bit. Everything the Bible says about the way we should respond to what we read about God can be summed up in the nine words of Psalm 29:2: 'Ascribe to the LORD the glory due to his name.' In a famous document written in the seventeenth century, the first question asked was, 'What is the chief end of man?' and the answer given was, 'To glorify God and to enjoy him for ever.' But how can we do this? God is glorious by nature, and we can no more make him glorious than we can make water wet. Nor can we add to his glory in any way, as he is infinitely and absolutely glorious. Neither can we reduce his glory in any way; as C. S. Lewis put it, 'A man can no more diminish God's glory by refusing to worship him than a lunatic can put out the sun by scribbling the word "darkness" on the walls of his cell.'

To ascribe to God the glory due to him is to worship him, recognizing that he has the prior claim on human life, and seeking to live in a way that draws attention to him. Floodlights are never used to draw attention to themselves, but to something else, often a significant building. God has placed you on this planet so that the quality of your life might draw attention not to yourself, but to him, and in that way to acknowledge his glory. In the Bible's words, you are to 'Let your light shine before others, so that they may see your good works and give glory to your Father who is in heaven' (Matthew 5:16 ).

How do you measure up? Can you honestly claim that your life draws attention to God? However highly you may think of yourself, the Bible's verdict in Romans 3:23 on humankind is crystal clear: 'All have sinned and fall short of the glory of God.' Whatever pressures you may be facing as you read this book, your greatest problem in life is not physical, mental, psychological or financial. It is not centred on your family, your other relationships, your job (or lack of one), your health or your bank balance. Irrespective of your age, culture or circumstances, your greatest problem is that by nature and from choice you are a self-centred rebel against God. However you may try to excuse it or cover it up, you have a moral and spiritual track record that does not measure up to God's perfect standards—and so do I.

The same is true for everyone. Left to ourselves we are all moral and spiritual wrecks of the glorious perfection in which our race was created. Our thoughts, words and actions constantly fall far short of reflecting the glory of our Creator, and 1 John 1:8 spells it out: 'If we say we have no sin, we deceive ourselves, and the truth is not in us.' You know perfectly well that you fall short of your own standards, let alone God's, however high or low you have set the bar. If you try to soften this by claiming to be living a fairly decent life, you run up against Jesus' statement that the most important of all God's commandments is, 'You shall love the Lord your God with all your heart and with all your soul and with all your mind and with all your strength' (Mark 12:30). Claiming that you have never fallen short of that benchmark is simply dishonest, and proof that you have, and the same is true for everybody. The knowledge that we are moral failures has been called, 'the truth that can't *not* be known.' As Charles Colson wrote, 'The knowledge of right and wrong is in us, and we know in our heart of hearts that we have not measured up.' This is why we have missed the meaning of what life is meant to be, and why we have no certainty about its true purpose.

Our failure and shame will be even worse on the day of judgement. When the England football team won the World Cup in 1966, the Queen presented the team's captain, Bobby Moore with the Jules Rimet Trophy. Asked by a reporter how he felt when going up to receive it, he said, 'It was terrifying, because as I was going up the steps to the balcony I saw that the Queen was wearing some beautiful white gloves. I looked at my hands and realized that they were covered in Wembley mud and I thought, "How can I shake hands with her like this?—I'll make her gloves dirty."' A film of the presentation shows him frantically wiping his hands on his shorts, trying his best to get rid of some of the mud and hoping that his hands would be clean enough. Facing an awesomely holy

God on the day of judgement will be much more serious. Are you hoping that you can wipe off enough of your life's 'mud' to make you able to face him with confidence, or with a clear conscience? Other people may speak well of you and commend your present behaviour and lifestyle, but their approval will count for nothing when you face a God who is 'majestic in holiness' (Exodus 15:11) and who has said that only people as perfect as those he first created can spend eternity with him in 'new heavens and a new earth' (2 Peter 3:13).

### TURN! TURN! TURN!

This means that if you are to have a right relationship with God, discover the purpose for which God created you and find the true meaning of life, things will have to change! Jesus made this clear in the first recorded words in his public ministry, recorded in Mark 1:15: 'The time is fulfilled, and the kingdom of God is at hand; *repent and believe in the gospel.*' Elsewhere, the Bible repeats this double-barrelled command and calls you to 'repentance towards God...and faith in our Lord Jesus Christ' (Acts 20:21). The remaining pages of this book will spell out what repentance and faith mean.

The word 'repentance' is not heard much today, yet without it nobody can have a right relationship with God. It is therefore vital that you understand its true meaning, which is much more than regret or self-pity.

**Firstly**, *it means a change of mind about sin.* It means realizing that no sin (not even those we think are 'small') can be shrugged off as just a weakness or a small error of judgement. Sin is never trivial, but always terrible, not a toy, but a tragedy. It is an offence against the majestic holiness of God. Sin brought God's curse on humanity, scarred the ecology of the whole universe, killed the only perfect man in human history, and separates us from God. If you truly repent, you will change your mind about sin.

**Secondly**, repentance means *a change of heart about sin.* It means realizing that sin defies God and defiles all sinners. Genuine repentance will leave you deeply ashamed because you have sinned against the one who died for you, and in doing so have deliberately broken the holy law of a loving God.

**Thirdly**, repentance means *a change of will about sin*. It is not enough to feel sorry that you have sinned, and it is much more than asking God to sweep your sins under the carpet. True sorrow for sin is marked by a deliberate change of direction. It means an honest longing and determination to live a new, God-centred life and not a self-centred one. Is this what you want? Repentance without turning away from sin is a contradiction in terms. If you truly repent, you will be able to lay hold of this promise found in 1 John 1:9: 'If we confess our sins, [God] is faithful and just to forgive us our sins and to cleanse us from all unrighteousness.'

Pulling all of this together, we can see that true repentance means a change of mind, a change of heart and a change of will about sin, leading to a new life, in which a person's views and values, affections and ambitions, motives and actions are no longer self-centred but God-centred. A person repenting does not suddenly become perfect, yet the change is so radical that C. S. Lewis called it going 'full speed astern.'

### 3D FAITH

As with repentance, faith involves the mind, the heart and the will. Firstly, *it involves the mind*: 'Without faith it is impossible to please [God], for whoever would draw near to God must believe that he exists and that he rewards those who seek him' (Hebrews 11:6). This is faith at its most basic. Do you believe that God exists? If you do, you have taken the first step of faith in finding him.

Basic faith also includes believing the Bible's testimony about Jesus. When his enemies challenged his claim to be God, Jesus replied, 'Unless you believe that I am he, you will die in your sins' (John 8:24). *What do you think of him?* Countless people go no further than accepting that he was a fine man, a great teacher or an influential example, but this gets nowhere near what is needed. As C. S Lewis famously put it, 'Either this man was, and is, the Son of God, or else a madman or something worse. You can shut him up for a fool, you can spit at him and kill him as a demon, or you can fall at his feet and call him Lord and God, but let us not come with any patronizing nonsense about his being a great human teacher. He has not left that open to us. He did not intend to.'

Secondly, biblical faith *involves the heart.* In Psalm 23:1 an Old Testament believer said, 'The Lord is *my* shepherd,' and one in the New Testament wrote in Galatians 2:20 of 'the Son of God, who loved *me* and gave himself for *me.*' Can you speak of Jesus in such a personal way?

Thirdly, faith in Jesus goes even further; *it involves the will.* It means committing yourself to him as your own personal Saviour. When you fly somewhere, it is not enough to have detailed and accurate information about the airline, or even to believe that the pilot is capable of flying you to your destination. You need to commit yourself to him by boarding the aircraft. In the same way, you need to commit your life to Jesus Christ, trusting him and him alone to save you from the guilt and consequences of your sin. This is the greatest need in your life, and until that issue is settled you will never lay hold on its true meaning and purpose. Jesus said 'I am the way, and the truth, and the life. No one comes to the Father except through me' (John 14:6). The way to get right with God is not by commitment to a programme, or to a principle, but to a person.

Have you repented towards God, admitting that you are a sinner and asking him to enable you to live in a way that is pleasing to him? Have you turned in faith to Jesus Christ, acknowledging him to be God and trusting him to save you from your sins and to transform your life? Only by doing so will your life gain the meaning and purpose God intended you to enjoy.

On 22 November 2013, fifty years after he died, a memorial stone to C. S. Lewis was dedicated in the floor of Poets' Corner in London's Westminster Abbey. It is inscribed with these words from one of his lectures: 'I believe in Christianity as I believe the sun has risen. Not only because I can see it but because by it I can see everything else.' Repentance and faith had brought him to that point.

## SEIZE THE DAY!

The day before the 9/11 terrorist attack in the United States in 2001, a passenger on an American Airlines domestic flight noticed a stewardess breaking up ice with a wine bottle. Concerned that she might hurt herself, he asked if there was some other way of doing this. The stewardess was impressed that he should be so concerned, and some time later she was glad to accept a Christian leaflet from him. Before the flight was over she told him it was the sixth leaflet of this kind she had been given recently, and asked him, 'What does God want from me?' The man replied 'Your life,' and then explained her need to get right with God through trusting Jesus Christ as her Saviour. Less than twenty-four hours later she was on the first plane to crash into New York's World Trade Centre. Your life may not come to such a violent and unexpected end, but however young or old you are it remains true that your days on earth 'pass away like smoke' (Psalm 102:3) and that your opportunity to get right with God is limited by circumstances over which you have no control.

One last thing—something you may never have heard before: *you will glorify God sooner or later.* In a stupendous statement about the life to come we are told that 'at the name of Jesus every knee should bow, in heaven and on earth and under the earth, and every tongue confess that Jesus Christ is Lord, to the glory of God the Father' (Philippians 2:10-11). One day every human being will join in agreeing that Jesus is who he says he is. Even those 'under the earth,' that is, who rejected the gospel while on earth and are to spend eternity in hell, will be forced to acknowledge this as they endure for ever their horrific fate. Hell has rightly been called 'truth seen too late.'

The Bible urges you, 'Seek the LORD while he may be found; call upon him while he is near' (Isaiah 55:6). It promises, 'Draw near to God, and he will draw near to you' (James 4:8). It assures you in Romans 6:23 that 'the free gift of God is eternal life in Christ Jesus our Lord.' Eternal life is not merely life that goes on for ever, but life in a living relationship with God that begins here and now and never ends. Why turn your back on all of this? Why would you deliberately choose to remain 'having no hope and without God in the world' (Ephesians 2:12)?

When Thomas, one of his followers, heard that Jesus had risen from the dead, he doubted whether this could possibly be true, but when Jesus appeared to him and gave him all the proof he needed, Thomas responded by saying, 'My Lord and my God' (John 20:28)! When you can say that to God with all your mind, heart and will, then you will have found the meaning of life.

Seize the day!